BEACH HOUSE BUSINESS MODEL

Airbnb Investing 101:
Finding, Optimizing, and Profiting
From Short-term and Vacation Rentals

Automated Retirees

TABLE OF CONTENTS

" Being rich is havig money;
being wealthy is having time"

Margaret Bonnano

Introduction

June 2017. I had graduated from college six months earlier and landed my "dream job."

And I absolutely hated it.

No one ever tells you about the sheer boredom adulthood brings. Or the deep fear you feel when you think about working in the same job for the next 40 years. Worse still, my parents and older relatives thought it was now *normal* to tell me things like, "Dang, I wish I could retire . . . just ten more years!" or "I'm not getting any younger!"

After you graduate, you begin realizing those things apply to you, too.

So, there I was, stuck in a job I'd spent the last four years focused on getting – and I couldn't imagine another 40 years of it. (Honestly, I couldn't even imagine another five years!)

Maybe you've come to this book for the very same reasons. You might *like* your job but want enough money to create a runway for yourself. Perhaps you're like me, and you believe your time is the most valuable asset you have; trading it for anything less than $1000 per hour is an outright travesty. Either way, I'm sure you found your way here like I did – by googling "how to kill my job."

There are several ways you can kill your job, but they all follow the same basic premise: create passive income. Most writers involved in the group known as the Automated Retirees have a mix of passive incomes to keep them diversified– everything from publishing books to trading stocks. *This* book aims to tell you about one specific type of passive income: Airbnbs.

Airbnbs attract me for a few reasons.

First, my goal is to kill my job by 2022 (#KMJ22), so I really can't afford to mess around or waste a lot of money. According to Smartasset.com, a 2/2 (two-bedroom, two-bathroom) vacation rental makes an average of $20,619 annually. That's a return I can get behind!

Second, I have always been attracted to real estate, a physical asset that typically appreciates over time. Who wouldn't want something like that? Still, I knew conventional rentals would not be right for me. After all, most investors make about $400 per month from those – pretty paltry numbers compared to the average Airbnb investor's returns.

Third, I like having vacation houses around the world. Investing in Airbnbs gives me the ability to take semi-free vacations, and I'm into that!

Fourth, I realized that I could automate this business's most annoying parts and hire out the rest. Passive income is the name of the game for me . . . I'm not trying to start huge business empires here.

But I have a different goal than the ones I hear from all the hyper-entrepreneurial and real estate investment podcasts. I don't harbor get-rich-quick ideas or adopt a "10x mentality" where I'd lie awake wondering how to pay my mortgage next month as a means of *forcing* myself to work hard. No, I have a different take on how I want to live my life. It's why I wrote this book.

I believe the only time we have is *right now*; we need to make our present time as pleasant as possible while shoring up for the future. So, yes, my goal is to retire in 2022, but I don't expect to become a bazillionaire – I simply want to replace my income and insurance expenses. My main concern isn't about becoming *rich*; I want to become *wealthy*. (Be sure to read the quote at the beginning of this chapter).

Having spent so many years working for someone else, I've come to understand the importance of time. Newsflash: Time is currency. When you go to work, you're trading your time for a piece of paper that you then exchange for someone else's time. Whether you're buying a house or a sandwich, you're outsourcing that task to someone else.

That's why I like passive income. It's like a cheat code; you're earning money by doing pretty much nothing. Sure, you put in a bit of work upfront (sweat equity), but then, it's smooth sailing from there. A passive income source (property) is set up, and it's like printing your own money . . . but *legal*.

Looking back on it now, I wish I's been one of those 17-year-olds on YouTube who skipped college and worked on creating a business. But you know what they say: **"The best time to plant a tree was 20 years ago. The second-best time is now."** *(Credited to an old Chinese proverb).*

So, let's plant some trees!

The Underground Millionaires Club

Fast forward a few months. I'm in Austin, Texas, sitting in some third-rate hotel's crowded, stuffy ballroom. The room is full of hundreds of investors – as far as the eye can see – sitting patiently, waiting for the meetup to start.

I'm not going to pretend this was some secret, elitist property society that meets to discuss lucrative investment portfolios. I mean, *really*, I found it on *meetup!* This meeting was just a bunch of regular real estate investors who were passionate about earning passive income.

Every meeting was very insightful, but that one night is the one that I credit to my current success. The topic at hand was one that I had previously discarded, thinking it wasn't *what all the other investors were doing,* so it probably *wasn't a good idea.* In fact, I almost didn't go that night.

Truthfully, the lessons I took away from that meeting changed the trajectory of my life. The topic was "Airbnbs Versus Rentals: Which One Is More Profitable?" To get a good debate going, the meeting facilitator split us into two groups: Those investing in (and swore by) traditional rentals and those currently investing in Airbnbs.

Where was I in this whole debate? Sitting silently in the back, gently tapping my fingers on my Notes app, sucking up all of the knowledge I could!

Investors in the long-term rental group were seasoned professionals. These guys either started investing during the 2007-2009 financial crisis and property crash (because houses were super cheap then) or had a substantial amount of wealth before the crash and then bought as many houses as they possibly could when inventory was plentiful and cheap.

During the crash, many people were forced to sell their homes. Most savvy investors saw this as a golden opportunity to buy as much property as they could. Since times were tough, there weren't as many investors then, so it was easier to find properties. Houses were also dirt cheap in Austin and around the US – we call that *discounted inventory* in real estate lingo.

It's much harder to get into mainstream real estate today (like flipping, renting, and wholesaling) because the houses just aren't as plentiful or as cheap as they were in 2009. There are also far more people investing in real estate now than there were back in the day, so the buyer's market for cheap houses is hugely oversaturated.

New investors need to find a way to work around that saturation, which is what Airbnb investing is all about! The Airbnb group investors were much newer to property investing, but dear lord, were they *ambitious!* They also had an air of calm about them that I just hadn't found with most mainstream investors. They weren't *always looking for that next deal* or *rushing to call a buyer...* more on that in a moment.

The Airbnb team consisted of two people: one we'll call *Sally*, and the other we'll call *Bob.*

Sally was a young lawyer in her 20s who owned four Airbnbs. She loved to travel, so she decided to buy Airbnbs in the tiny towns she enjoyed traveling to.

Bob was an older man in his 60s and had been investing in Airbnbs "full time" for the past two years. From the beginning, he'd seen how huge Airbnbs could be, and he was considered an early adopter. He took a different approach than Sally - paying for all the data that Mashvisor had and paying a data scientist to find *the best investments.*

One of the key topics of the night was the competitiveness of the markets. The mainstream investors went first. They mostly talked about how – back in the good old days – you could buy a house with a balance transfer and a 0% APR credit card.

In other words, back in 2007, you *literally* did not need any money to buy a house.

Of course, that's not an option now – but they sure did talk a lot about it! They would complain about how they could only manage to find a house or two every few months and that mailer expenses were off the charts. If their goal was to turn me off of long-term rentals, they definitely did their job.

Next came the Airbnb debaters: good old Bob and Sally. They talked about the competitive market like it was not a big deal. In fact, Bob often overpaid when he bought an investment because he wanted to make sure that he won the contract.

After all, this was when houses were being sold within ten days of being on the market – for $10,000 more than the asking price. I had even heard stories of sellers asking their potential buyers to write letters about how they would be using the house after the sale. Absolutely crazy!

Guess that didn't matter when one Airbnb would bring you $20,000 per year! Heck, Bob even had enough left over to hire a short-term rental management company. He, literally, didn't have to do *anything* except look at his bank account each month and bask in its glory.

Sally, the lawyer, used her time to talk about her investment strategies. She loved to travel, so her strategy was to buy Airbnb investment properties in places where she wanted to travel – kind of like a vacation home that someone else paid for!

She said that since much of her properties' management was automated, it only took an hour or less each week to check up on the Airbnbs. She was very shrewd and only had about four properties, so she had decided to manage them herself… even though all of them were hundreds of miles away.

The next subject interested me a lot: wear and tear. Surely it would take more to keep up an Airbnb than it would a long-term rental. After all, the wear and tear on those houses must be much worse since they are a revolving door of vacationers.

When the rental team spoke about wear and tear, they laughed about a few instances when they'd had a terrible tenant who wouldn't leave; some had to be evicted. Sometimes, their tenants destroyed the property past the point that the deposit would pay for the damages. I'd heard all these stories before, but there was something about hearing it *this* time – juxtaposed with the Airbnb team – that really bothered me because . . .

When it was the Airbnb team's turn to speak, they looked at each other, and then Sally talked about one time when one of her guests broke a toilet. She filed a claim with Airbnb and was given twice the amount of money needed for a new one. I don't know why that toilet story is what did it for me; you'd think the profits would have been enough, but no . . . it was a story about a toilet.

More Than a Passing Trend

After attending that meeting, I was more determined than ever to commit to investing in homes and turning them into Airbnbs. I had $15,000 in my savings account – *a lot* for most twenty-somethings – and I intended to use it as a sort of nest egg for my early retirement. I found a bank that would accept a 10% down payment for an investment property and set out on a mission to find the perfect Airbnb "Pinterest-approved" house.

I am all about finding the easiest ways to do things and automating as many systems as possible. My blog, www.AutomatedRetirees.com, helps hopeful investors set up additional income streams so they can start their path towards early retirement.

Though I wrote the intro, the book is written from the experience of five up-and-coming Airbnb investors. Some of us have more experience than others, but we'd like to think of ourselves as just a couple of average Joes who are a few steps ahead of you.

That means that we still understand your mindset, which could range from hesitant to full-blown panic! As a collective, we have a fresh experience with the beginner issues you're going to face – and experience with problems you'll face down the road. Think of us as your pocket property mentors, preparing you for your life-long journey into this exhilarating industry.

Now, let's get started, shall we?

16

Download a Free Copy of The Complete Done For You Suite To Supercharge Your First Investment!

Do you want me to hand you all of the resources I use in my business? This *Done For You Suite* will save you hours of time because it includes everything you need to get started profiting from Airbnb.

Furnish and Accessorize your Airbnb (On the Cheap)

Do you want the shopping list I use when I furnish a new Airbnb? Well, this is it! From the best bed frame to the exact set of floating knives, this is what I use to cheaply furnish my Airbnbs.

Automated Consumables Shopping List

Airbnb is in the hospitality business. You're going to need to buy your guest certain consumables like shampoo, coffee grounds, and cleaning supplies. This list has everything you need to buy your guests and a handy guide on how to automate the purchase process.

5 Star Review Messaging Template

Getting 5-star reviews is a very important part of being a successful Airbnb host. Since we are in the hospitality industry, we need to be hospitable to get that stellar review! One way to do this is to have a messaging template set up so that every guest feels like you care about them. Allow me cut out all the work of figuring out what to say and just give you the one I use.

Complete Guidebook Template

Your guests need to know quite a few things about the area they chose to stay. Where are the best restaurants? What are the rules of the house? How do they turn on that one shower that was probably designed by an alien? My guidebook gives you a basic template and walks you through the process of creating one for each of your properties. That way, your guests will know everything there is to know (without texting you!)

Cleaning Crew Turn-Over and Yearly Checklist

If you choose to hire a cleaning crew (or even clean yourself) you will need a turn over checklist to ensure that your property is clean as a whistle. But cleaning an Airbnb is not like cleaning your house. You need to be detailed, disinfect certain surfaces you might not think of, and have a plan on how to clean your property as fast as possible. That's where my *Cleaning Crew Turn-Over and Yearly Checklist* comes in! Not only do I tell you exactly what to clean every visit, I also tell you what you need to clean once a year to maintain luxury resort standards.

Airbnb City Comping Spreadsheet

To bnb or not to bnb; that is the question. How do you know which city will be profitable for your business? I go over very detailed steps later on in the book, but this spreadsheet really helps you organize it! Make sure you download it so that you can have a very organized experience while finding the best place to invest.

To download all of these for free, go to www.AutomatedRetirees.com/Airbnb

CHAPTER

Why Airbnb Investing Is THE FASTEST Way to Retire Early

"A big part of financial freedom is having your heart and mind free from worry about the what-ifs of life."

Suze Orman

What You Can Expect in This Chapter:

- *An in-depth look at what the Airbnb hype is all about—is it just a trend?*

- *A discussion about the benefits of being a short-term rental host on Airbnb.*

- *Did you know there are various ways to start an Airbnb with as little as $10,000? Well, I'll share my insights on those, too!*

- *If you're not sold already, I'll discuss a few other advantages and disadvantages you should consider.*

It All Started With an Air Mattress...

Air Bed and Breakfast was started in 2007 by innovators Brian Chesky and Joe Gabbia. They had just moved to San Francisco from New York, so they were used to the idea of fully booked hotels and expensive housing options. One weekend, they noticed that all the area hotels were booked due to a very popular conference.

Chesky and Gabbia saw this as an opportunity to start a company offering accommodations that would compete directly with hotels. In this case, it wouldn't be challenging because the demand for hotels greatly exceeded the supply.

However, they didn't have five-star luxury suites in mind. No, they were just going to offer an air mattress and a warm breakfast in their apartments. Air Bed and Breakfast's popularity grew from that time forward, eventually morphing into the company we all know and love today: Airbnb.

If you've ever stayed at an Airbnb, you know that nowadays, people are offering much more than *three hots and a cot*. It has become a full and busy industry! One where you can rent an entire home for just over the price of a hotel room. That's the type of vacation that I can get behind!

The Craze Over Airbnb

Like I alluded to in my opening, most investors think Airbnb's popularity is a passing fad. In reality, short-term vacation rentals are only growing in popularity!

The Air Bed and Breakfast app was launched in 2007 and initially was a means to help the founders afford to pay their rent (how ironic!) By 2011, Airbnb was present in 89 countries, and the platform had booked over one 1 million nights.

By 2015, those numbers soared; Airbnb was available in 190 countries and had close to 40 million nights booked. I'm sure you're wondering what the stats are for the year 2020 – let's just say they are *mind-blowing!* Airbnb is currently in 220 countries and has over 2 million people staying in an Airbnb *every night*. That's even with the new coronavirus pandemic restrictions in place!

That doesn't sound like a fad to me; that sounds like a movement.

When the company started, it had a massive reach on Craigslist, providing the platform with the necessary exposure it needed. Of course, posting your Airbnb listing on Craigslist is no longer allowed, but that's okay because I highly doubt anyone would take you up on it anyway!

That begs the question, why does a traveler feel safer using Airbnb than Craigslist? If they're trying to avoid risk, wouldn't they just pay a hotel's premium price? If it's about money, motels have a decent reputation, and some cost only $49.99 per night.

1. Airbnb Review System

Airbnb has a fantastic review system where both the host and the guest review each other. Neither sees the review from the other until after it has been posted, so it's pretty fair in that regard.

These reviews help the platform in two ways. First, the guests know which Airbnb to avoid. Anyone can put lipstick on a pig and dress up a home for photos, but making sure the home is safe, clean, and smells great for every guest – every time – is a whole other ballgame. The reviews also give the guests a lot of useful information like "is this neighborhood safe?" "does the host bother you all the time?" "Is the hot tub at the perfect temperature?" These sorts of questions/answers can be crucial to a new guest, so they often take to the review section to make sure they're getting a good deal for their money.

You're a host, so obviously, this means that you need to be on top of your game to get 5-star reviews. *(Don't worry; we'll go over increasing your chances to get 5-star reviews later on.)*

Similar to hosts, guests also get reviewed. This should seriously excite you as a host because it means you are less likely to have a nightmare guest. You know the ones . . . they show up early, leave late, and wreck your house. While these types of guests aren't non-existent, they are becoming rarer and rarer; you can thank honest reviews for that.

2. Affordability and Adventure

Airbnb appeals to frequent travelers, adventure-seekers, and millennials because they are affordable and give you a sense of adventure. After all, who could resist living like a local for less than the price of living like a tourist?

Sometimes, travelers just need a place to crash. Some people want to travel on the cheap and just need a place to put their stuff. They'd rather spend their money on experiences than accommodations.

Also, lots of tourists travel in huge groups. These gigantic groups favor Airbnbs over traditional hotels because it's cheaper and it feels more intimate. Your group isn't in a hotel where there are stringent rules and regulations, or other guests. You're in your own space.

3. The Concept Is So Unique

Part of the buzz around Airbnb is due to the novelty of it. Before Airbnb, it was kind of impractical to find a safe place to stay when you went on vacation or business. Airbnb also opens you up to unique spaces like mansions, houseboats, treehouses, igloos, and barns! Try finding one of those that didn't look sketchy on Craigslist back in 2006!

This was a much different experience than staying at a hotel. Traditional hotel rooms are standardized. Sure, there are suites and penthouses, but you'd have to blow a fat wad of cash to crash there. Airbnb is much less expensive and easily shared amongst friends when the property is high-priced. Could you imagine renting out a mansion with 20 of your closest friends?

4. Airbnb Supports a Free Market

The cost of staying a night or weekend at a fully decked-out Airbnb home is usually less than what you would pay if you stayed at a traditional hotel for the same time.

Running a hotel is much more expensive than running a single-family home. You have a front desk, maids, pool cleaners... the list goes on and on - not to mention that this is usually their full-time job!

Between the real estate fees and the staff salaries, running a hotel is an expensive business– much more expensive than hiring a maid as a contractor to come to clean the house every three to seven days (especially when you pass most of this expense on to the customer!)

This gives Airbnb properties a certain level of flexibility with their pricing that hotels just don't have. Besides, some people don't care if a maid comes to clean their room every day or if they have to make a bed; they just need a safe, warm place to stay for a night. Airbnb caters to this part of the market and is a great way to compete with hotel pricing.

Before Airbnb was invented, there were only a few big players in the travel and accommodation market. Sure, you could choose between a Motel 6, a Hilton, or a Ritz, but honestly, what you picked and the level of service you were afforded was very dependent on your price point.

Airbnb opened the market to average, everyday people who may only have a spare couch to share. Anyone could list their house on Airbnb to make a little bit of cash. That not only supports the free market, it also means that anyone could get paid for being a hotel!

Some might just opt to rent out one of their spare bedrooms while others (like us!) will turn it into a full-blown investment. The options are endless! And we can all get a little slice of that pie instead of it being relegated to massive hotel chains who either ignore you completely or charge you an arm and a leg!

The Benefits of Being a Short-Term Rental Host

If you own your house and have been trying to find a way to set up a semi-passive stream of income, then Airbnb is an excellent possibility. Renting your space on Airbnb is easy, and finding a spare area to rent can be even easier! Yes, many people rent out an entire house but, hailing back to Airbnb's roots, some hosts simply rent an air mattress or couch in their living room. I guarantee you that there is at least one person out of the 150 million users on the platform who wants to travel to your area and is looking for a space like yours.

If you're like Sally (the lawyer from the intro), maybe you want to buy a vacation home, but you don't have the money to let it just sit there. You need some other way to pay for it. My family likes to visit Florida every year; we'd save thousands if we just had a vacation home there! ;-)

Airbnb is great for vacation homes, too (or even your own home if you go on vacation). You don't need to rent your property out all year; you can schedule when it is unavailable. So, if you like to visit Florida the second week of July each year, you can mark that week as unavailable and use your vacation home *as a vacation home*!

The icing on the cake: if you want to list your *real* home on Airbnb for the second week of July while you're visiting your vacation home, you can do that too! Yep, you can double-dip, using your full-time home as a moneymaker, renting it out during popular festivals or tourist times.

I live in Austin, where one of the main attractions is ACL (Austin City Limits). All I have to do is choose to take a vacation that week, and *voila!* My house becomes a cash cow. *(I've seen people in Austin make as much as $10,000 from that single week.)*

You might be concerned about the amount of work you will need to put in as an excellent short-term rental host. Like any business, you will need to put in some sweat equity, but eventually, it all pays off. This is all about making the income as passive as possible.

How to Start an Airbnb With $10,000

You don't need to be a millionaire to invest in Airbnb. In fact, you should search for properties with a down payment of no more than $10,000.

The reason that real estate is so lucrative is that you can *leverage your money*. Put another way; you can take out a loan for a portion of what the house is worth instead of using cash to buy it outright– called *investing in the spread*. So, as long as you make money, it doesn't matter how expensive your loan is. If you're paying $1300 for a house each month, but you make $2000, then you're successfully investing in the spread.

Many new investors don't think about investing in the spread. They often believe they need to be somewhat rich to make any sizeable amount of money. Sadly, these types often believe (incorrectly) that the rich have no debt and use cash to pay for everything; they couldn't be further from the truth. The rich are rich because they understand how to use debt, not money!

Debt is the reason why 90% of new millionaires make their money through investing in real estate. You can turn $10,000 into a $700 per month stream of income and a tangible property. Sure, you can take out the same loan and throw it all in the stock market as well, but that's so risky that only a few crazy people do it! And I certainly don't recommend it if you've never invested in stocks before. Real estate is much more forgiving - at least you have a tangible asset in the end.

So, how do you find and buy an investment property with only $10,000? In 2019, banks started taking a closer look at Airbnbs as investment properties. While they aren't your primary home, they remain valuable properties if kept in excellent condition. Some Airbnbs are nicer than the houses that people live in! That's great for the banks because they are investing in you when they give you a loan. If you stop paying, they need to repossess the property, aka *foreclose*. Banks have little interest in foreclosing on properties in which they'll lose money; they only want to foreclose on great properties they can turn around and sell. Once banks realized that Airbnbs are well-maintained, they started offering more advantageous loans.

Of course, your credit score and the bank you choose dictate exactly how much you need for a down payment, but normally they only need 10%. For $100,000, that's $10,000. Of course, you will have to pay some closing fees, so really, you'll want to shoot for a down payment of $7000, but you get the gist. The more money you have for your down payment, the more you can pay for a house, and the easier it will be to find one.

But where do we find these cheap properties? That is the one-hundred-thousand-dollar question, isn't it? It takes a little bit of work (and quite a bit of internet sleuthing), but you can find these properties pretty much anywhere. Me? I prefer the tiny beach and mountain towns because I know that travelers love to explore them. That's why this book is called *Beach House Business Model*.

Of course, you can use my sleuthing method to find an investment property that fits your budget anywhere; as for me, I like staying somewhere "for free" when I'm on vacation!

How to Get $10,000

I am not an adherent to the *ZERO DOLLAR DOWN!* investment strategies that you might see floating around the internet. I strongly recommend that you have a minimum of $10,000 saved up because I think that's the sweet spot for a down payment on an investment property that is both affordable and nice.

But if you don't have any money at all, don't worry, I got you covered. To some of you, saving $10,000 might seem like a monumental task, but it isn't! You just need to have the right attitude and the tenacity to get it done. In fact, there are some creative ways you can use Airbnb to make your $10,000 investment before you even have an investment property!

The first step in doing something is believing you can. Know that other people are using these very same methods to make and save some money. You are no different than them; they just wake up every day and decide that they're going to make their dreams come true. In fact, you might be smarter, a harder worker, or savvier than the average joe!

If you own your own home, then you can, of course, use the information that I give you in this book to rent part of it on Airbnb. It should be, more or less, the same process. But if you want a more in-depth look at making money with your own home or even a guide to buying one that is conducive to renting parts of it out without losing your mind, then my book *How To Live For Free* will be an excellent asset for you.

If you don't have your own house, then I still have great news for you! You don't need your *own* property to invest in Airbnb; you can just start *arbitraging!* Arbitrage is when you pay retail price for something and then sell it piecemeal for a higher price. It's pretty much how Walmart makes all their money. You don't just have to do this with cheap inventory, though; you can do this with anything, including rentals. Rental arbitrage is when you rent a property from a landlord, and then you rent their property to *other people* for a higher price. It's pretty much textbook *investing in the spread.*

So, how would this work on Airbnb? Let's say you find a beautiful condo going for $500 per month, and you decide to list it on Airbnb for $60 per night. If you had even a 50% occupancy rate(which is very low!), you'd have enough to pay your rent *and* yourself.

With this method, you don't own the property, but you partner with someone who does. It's different than managing it because you are technically renting out their property, so you are responsible for paying the landlord each month. But trust me, a lot more can go right than wrong.

Rental arbitrage is legal and used successfully by thousands of new investors, but it does require consent and partnership with a landlord. This is usually the first hurdle that you'll have to jump over to successfully negotiate a rental arbitrage situation. Speaking with landlords is an art and having the right mindset to take all of the rejection is a skill.

This is exactly what my latest no-frills, straight-to-the-point book *No Property No Problem* is about. I highly recommend it. And, if you choose to rent out someone else's property on Airbnb, then you'll make all of the mistakes new Airbnb investors make on someone else's dime. Win-win!

The Good, the Bad and the Ugly of Becoming a Host on Airbnb (The Unfiltered Truth)

I hope you're at least warming up to the idea of investing in Airbnbs instead of conventional real estate! But, like me, I know you probably want to go into this business with your eyes wide open. There's a lot of money to be made by investing in Airbnbs, but there are some pitfalls that you need to watch out for as well.

As much as I would like to pretend that there is no downside, that wouldn't be honest. Below is a sort of explanation of the pros and cons of investing in Airbnbs.

Nonetheless, with all the cons presented, I still believe that Airbnb investing is still one of the best ways to get your feet wet in the rental business.

Let's Start With the Bad News...

Fluctuating Income

Yes, income through Airbnb tends to fluctuate, and investing in beach or mountain towns can have the most significant ebb and flow due to on-and-off (high and low) seasons. That said, investing in *any* town comes with variability. Thankfully, you can plan for this and choose to only invest in cities where the heavy seasons are more than enough to cover your expenses for the year; light seasons become the icing on the cake.

When we look at potential investment towns, we can estimate our overall income and expenditure for the year. So, don't panic! There's an easy way to plan for the light season so that you have more than enough money to cover it.

I also will share several strategies you can use when entering light seasons; these will keep your bookings high. Stay tuned!

Cleaning Up

Your guests expect your Airbnb to be hotel-quality clean, so you will need to have it spotless after every guest leaves. Like everything in the business world, there are a few ways you can handle this. By far, the cheapest way is to clean it yourself. If you choose to buy an Airbnb nearby and have the time to run over and clean it at noon on a random Tuesday, then this might be the perfect option for you!

If you don't have that kind of free time, then you'll need to hire a maid – and not just *any* kind of maid. You'll need one that knows to wash all the sheets, take note of missing consumables, and a host of other tasks. Fortunately, many maid services specializing in vacation rentals have sprung up over the last few years; you should find it relatively easy to locate a service that cleans your Airbnb to perfection. Using a company specializing in STRs is the most expensive route –and by far the least time-consuming. After all, they have a staff who handle scheduling the cleaning, training the maids, and replacing no-shows.

If you want a middle-of-the-road option, you can hire and train a team of maids yourself. While this is usually cheaper than using an Airbnb maid service, it is more time-consuming because *you* are now responsible for scheduling the cleaning, training new staff, and replacing no-shows.

No matter who you hire, you should have a maid checklist. I've included mine in the Done For You Suite you got at the beginning of the book. This guide tells your maids what they need to focus on for each room, and though your specific list may be slightly different, much of it will be similar to mine. After all, most houses are built relatively the same – and get dirty in pretty much the same ways.

Ask your maids to take pictures of anything they think is broken and request that they let you know when to restock your Airbnb. If you have a locked area in your house that only the maids can access, you can hook up an Amazon button for all of the consumables you need to buy, saving you loads of time. This automates the restocking process for your Airbnb (I've included directions on how to purchase those buttons in my *Done For You Suite: Automated Consumables Shopping List* as well.)

No matter how you slice it, someone is getting paid for cleaning your house because Airbnb lets you charge each guest a one-time cleaning fee. If you want to clean the house, you can pocket that money just as easily as any maid!

Possible Annoying Guests

Every guest on Airbnb is vetted and reviewed. Unlike traditional hotels, where the doors are open to anyone and everyone, Airbnb gives you the option to review guest profiles and ask them questions before agreeing to their booking.

If you do end up with a bad guest, there are ways you can mitigate some of the issues. For instance, if they break any of your rules, you can kick them out. Airbnb also gives you up to a million dollars in insurance if anything is broken or stolen. Remember my toilet story?

The cherry on top: Airbnb allows you to rate every guest that books your property. If you get a lousy guest, you can give them a 1-star rating, dramatically reducing their chances of ever getting booked at any other Airbnb property in the future. I'm a big believer in Lady Karma, and I have no problem helping her give people what they deserve!

Bad Reviews Happen to the Best of Us

If you've ever worked in the service industry, you know that people will take off a star (or five) for seemingly no reason.

No matter how comfortable you make your guests' stay, there will always be those few who are unsatisfied with their experience. You simply cannot please everybody; if most of your reviews are great, then one sour apple won't hurt you. I can assure you that one or two poor reviews once in a while are not the end of the world. Need an example? Look at the review section of this book!

Okay, Now for the Good News...

Extra Money – You get to earn extra money every month, which is the whole point, right? My entire strategy is to create so many passive income streams that even if one of them fails, the others pick up the slack. After all, most millionaires have seven streams on average! (I've got to pump my numbers up because I only have three!)

Eventually, you'll have so many Airbnbs that you will feel comfortable branching out into a new passive stream of income or maybe even quitting your job before you diversify. Either way, more money is a great thing.

Flexible Calendar

Airbnb allows you to have a flexible calendar, blocking off days or weeks you may want to use the property. Guests will only be able to book days that you have left open on Airbnb.

If you have other properties that are usually rented out long-term but have been vacant, you can use Airbnb to fill them temporarily. Just make sure you don't allow guests to book out more than one month ahead; this way, you can go back to renting long-term when you find someone to rent your property (if you even want to!)

Insurance Included

Airbnb also offers you property insurance against any theft or damages by guests. This provides you with the security to host guests without having to panic about your valuables being stolen – or any other worst-case scenario.

I will warn you that this insurance policy does not cover jewelry or TVs, so make sure you move all your personal jewelry into a locked safe (if it's your own home) and mount all TVs to the wall, so they aren't simple to remove. TV and jewelry thefts don't happen often, but it's best to mitigate these risks as much as possible.

Easy-to-Use Platform

Airbnb does a lot of the heavy lifting for you. Its smart platform offers you an affordable way to advertise your property, take payments, and make bookings through the website. Most of the manual processes, such as making a phone reservation or sending guests email invoices, are handled through the platform. Airbnb streamlines the entire advertising, booking, and payment process, a win/win for you and your guests.

TL;DR

(Too long; didn't read. A section for those of us who like to 3x our Youtube videos.)

Airbnb is dominating the worldwide short-term rental market. While it's almost impossible to time the market (and with so much economic instability), now is the best time to make sure you have some extra cash if your regular income falls through. I am a big believer in being self-sufficient. Real estate is one way you can ensure you and your family are always taken care of.

Becoming a host on Airbnb is pretty straightforward. All you need is a decent home or a space you can rent out to travelers, businesspeople, or those looking for short-term rental.

Even if you don't have a space of your own, you can partner with a landlord and rent out their property. If you have even a small amount of money (say, $7-10K), you can buy a house using the power of debt. The options are endless! So, what are you waiting for? Let's get started...

CHAPTER

The Two BEST Airbnb Investments

"Wide diversification is only required when investors do not understand what they are doing."

~ Warren Buffett

What You Can Expect in This Chapter:

- *How to choose the best investment property for 100% occupancy*

- *Financing your investment*

- *Is there such a thing as the "perfect location?"*

Who Said You Need to Settle?

Self-help gurus rave about giving up Starbucks and canceling your Netflix account so you can *live the entrepreneurial way* and be 100% focused on your goals. Yes, I'll admit it, I gave this a try for a few months and found that *that* kind of life isn't for me.

I look at life as a big, fantastic journey where you have to balance work with play. So, if I can't be a successful entrepreneur *and* watch Gordan Ramsay help a struggling restaurant owner regain their zeal for cooking every day, maybe I don't want success!

Kidding . . . kidding . . . Well, okay – not really!

Gordan Ramsay actually helped me too. I had spent three weeks agonizing over where I was going to buy my first Airbnb property. My town's real estate prices were out of my price range, and all the small towns nearby had less than stellar occupancy rates.

Here, I was dealing with a "nice life problem"—I had my deposit ready to secure my first Airbnb home, but I couldn't find my ideal property or location. Okay, I'll admit it: My standards were high, but heck, who said I needed to settle?

I had two primary criteria that needed to be met: My property had to be in an area with high demand and low competition. Easier said than done, right? I spent the next three weeks browsing Mashvisor (in short, an almost worldwide data aggregation site for short term rentals). I wanted to find the perfect location for my first Airbnb. I hadn't told anyone I was looking to invest in real estate yet, so it was just me –going solo.

I wasn't having much success aimlessly searching the United States on Mashvisor until one night when I decided to take a break and watch Gordan Ramsay help a struggling restaurant in a small beach town.

They always start the show the same way: some B-roll footage of the restaurant, a couple of terrible testimonials from the restaurant workers, and, of course, the location. I'd seen the beginning a hundred times, but this time was different. This time, the name of the small Florida town caught my attention.

"I should check that small town and see what the Airbnb situation is like..."

It turns out, Gordan Ramsay helps more than just struggling restaurateurs – he also helps newbie Airbnb investors! I immediately logged onto Redfin and started browsing the local housing inventory.

I called on my trusted team of expert assistants (my husband and my dad), and we all made arrangements to fly down to Florida so we could see each property in person. This would be my first real estate purchase outside of my own house, so I wanted to see it with my own eyes (and smell it with my own nose!)

We went through each of the houses and got a good ~~whiff~~ look. I decided only to buy homes and condos that didn't need much work. The newer, the better! For me, the *easier* the purchase, the better. Besides, the Airbnb profits are so good that you don't have to worry about finding trash and turning it into treasure.

A few months later, I had the keys to my first full-on investment property.

Tips on Securing a High Income Property That Will Attract Tourists

Over the past decade, the rise of short-term rentals has influenced how property investors define an *attractive* property. A new wave of investors has taken the leap, choosing to invest in Airbnbs.

However, even after an investor has made up their mind about going the Airbnb route, many still get confused about which property type will rake in the most income. The debate is usually between purchasing an Airbnb house or an Airbnb condo.

The list below touches on a few reasons why opting for an Airbnb condo is the better choice (especially for newbie property investors).

1. Condos Tend to Be Cheaper

One of the most attractive benefits of purchasing a condo is that it tends to be much cheaper than purchasing a house. It's a lot easier to find an affordable condo in a prime location than buying a house in the same market.

Even if the condo looks a bit outdated, if it's in a great location, you can always spruce it up, equipping it with all the amenities a traveler needs. The trick is spending as little as possible while not settling for anything sub-par. Buying a condo will allow you to do this, generating the same amount of income (if not just a little less) as an Airbnb house.

2. Condo Prices Appeal to More Guests

Almost every property investor has the same goal: to generate as much income as possible in the shortest time. Likewise, every tourist has a goal: spending as little as possible on their accommodations so that they have more money to spend on making memories.

These two parties need to reach an understanding for both to agree to a transaction. Most of the time, this understanding is determined by the price. That's where a condo shines!

Not only can condos be located in *the heart of downtown* (more often than houses), condos take up less space, so they are generally cheaper to purchase. Let's connect those dots: If they're cheaper to purchase, you can charge less. And if you can charge less, it makes it easier to find a property that fits your preferred profit margin.

3. Condos Offer More Convenience

As beautiful as your home may be, most of your guests will spend their days out of the house, exploring local thrills. It's kind of rare for a guest to go on vacation, pay for an Airbnb and not venture out into the surrounding area! It's easier to find a condo that is right there, in the middle of the action, than it is to find a house (Bonus points for a *breathtaking* view).

Guests also don't have to worry about security because most condos have CCTVs or security guards on standby. That gives guests peace of mind when they are exploring an unfamiliar town.

4. A House is More Maintenance

Airbnb *houses* are a lot more expensive to maintain. Depending on the actual size, it may cost you a lot to keep your house clean and fully operational. The maintenance cost increases even more when you have a large garden or outdoor area requiring regular maintenance.

A condo, on the other hand, is easier to clean and maintain. The grounds are usually taken care of by your HOA dues, and common areas (like hallways) are cleaned meticulously. Yes, you do pay for these services, but I can almost guarantee you that they will make the grounds more beautiful than you could – and you don't even have to coordinate it.

5. Other Airbnb Investors Stay Away From Them

The condo question is one often debated in the Airbnb community: *To condo or not to condo?* Since I like to invest mainly in tourist destinations, condos provide an excellent investment, especially since I try to find small towns that lean towards less regulation.

Some investors don't want to deal with the hassle of an HOA. But to those investors, I say: houses have HOAs too! Home HOAs can change just as quickly as condo HOAs; it's flawed reasoning to refuse condo investments because they have an HOA.

Because other investors tend to stay away from them, it opens the market up for us! We can set ourselves apart by giving our renters fantastic views in great locations. So, to those investors who agree, I say, *condo on*!

A Quick Note

As mentioned, like houses, condos have HOAs. It's extra crucial for you to read the HOA bylaws before signing a contract with a condo because they are more likely to tell you that you <u>cannot</u> use the property for short-term rentals. Sometimes, you can convince them that you will be a great host and win that exception, but you'll have to fire up your negotiation skills and deliver on your promises! Keep that in mind when you go on the hunt.

Your New Tools

Finding the information is extremely easy now that we have data aggregators that pull directly from Airbnb, VRBO, and other short-term rental C2C (consumer-to-consumer) companies.

We'll talk more about how to use these services later, but as a sneak peek, there's Airdna (US only), Mashvisor (worldwide), and Airbnb.com itself! I'll show you the general flow that I use for these tools later on, but generally, they can give you all the information you need; it becomes a matter of how much you want to spend versus how much time you have!

The Ins and Outs of Financing

It's a good idea to start with at least $15,000 saved up and ready to spend on your first Airbnb property ($10,000 for the down payment and $5,000 in reserve in a 0% APR credit card). Remember our earlier discussion (Chapter 1) about leveraging loans? Well, this is where that information becomes essential.

Due to the time value of money, the best loan is one where you have a low interest rate and a lot of time to repay it.

I recommend you try to find a loan before purchasing a house because the banks will preapprove you for a certain amount based on your credit score. This preapproved amount will determine how much you need for your down payment, how much your interest rate will be, and other key terms. It will also allow you to compare the rates between banks/credit unions so you can pick the best one.

When searching for the right loan, visit as many banks and credit unions as you can in 14 days. Why 14 days? Each bank you visit will perform a hard inquiry on your account. A few hard inquiries don't affect a credit score, but any more than three, and they will start to damage it. Still, the three major credit bureaus (Equifax, Experian, and Transunion) understand that people need to go loan shopping to find the best loan. After all, that's how the free market works. So, they made a rule: all hard inquiries performed within a 14-day period only count as one inquiry.

When you go to the bank, you have several things to talk about; a critical question they'll ask is whether your property will be used as a vacation home or as an investment property.

I want to caution you here. You shouldn't lie to a bank to get a better rate. If they find out that you lied to them, they can call their loan to terms and make you pay off the entire thing immediately – just like that! That's enough to cause most people to foreclose!

However, if you plan to use this home as a vacation home and rent it out on Airbnb part-time, you can technically answer the bank in the affirmative to their vacation home question. Remember, I'm not a lawyer, and I'm not here to give you legal advice, so make sure to consult a legal expert to make your best decisions!

To answer that question legally, it's crucial to ensure that the property meets all second home criteria before approaching the lender. Some of the criteria most lenders look out for include:

- The owner must occupy the property for at least a portion of the year.

- The property is a one-unit home, not a duplex, triplex, or four-plex.

- The property is suitable to be used throughout the year.

- The property belongs exclusively to the buyer.

- The property is not rented on a full-time basis or under any time-share arrangement.

- The property is not operated by a property management firm that controls occupancy (a third-party company.)

Simply put: if you are going to go this route, make sure you're telling them the truth!

Why go through all this trouble of classifying your property as a vacation home? Well, because you might end up getting a better interest rate and a lower required down payment. I say, *shoot for 10%.*

Heads-up, though. If your down payment is less than 20%, you may be asked to pay mortgage insurance until it gets to 20%. This usually increases your monthly payment by $50 to $150 – which is entirely reasonable. Sure, you'll pay a bit extra on the loan, but you'll be able to leverage your money much further if you only have to have a 10% down payment instead of 20%.

There are other financing options available to you. Depending on your particular situation, you can use any of the short-term rental financing options listed below to purchase your first investment property.

1. Quicken Loans Vacation Rental Mortgages

One of the most clean-cut and viable finance options for buying your Airbnb property is a vacation mortgage loan from Quicken Loans, which offers fixed-rate loans with payment periods between 8 and 30 years.

You could pay as little as 10% for a down payment on your property with flexible monthly repayments. To qualify for this type of loan, you would still need good credit (a credit score of 620+), but the interest rates are almost the same as conventional loans—the only difference is that these loans are explicitly for vacation rentals.

That means that instead of a 2.75% interest rate, you might just get a 3.25% interest rate. (Those were my actual numbers in 2020!) In the grand scheme of things, this rate isn't that bad, especially when you compare it to a personal loan (5%+) or a hard money loan (8-18%).

2. Home Equity Loans or Home Equity Line of Credit (HELOC)

Another way you can finance your Airbnb property is with a home equity loan. Of course, you can only use HELOCs if you already own a property because you are setting up a second mortgage to "cash out" on your current home.

HELOCs put a lien on the property you are mortgaging; if you can't repay the loan, the bank can foreclose on it.

Why would anyone do this? For starters, HELOCs' interest rate is generally much lower than any interest rate you can get from a bank on another house. Investors also use HELOCs as a way to get money for their properties without selling them.

Let's look at an example. Say you find an SFR (single-family residence) for $200,000, and you can't find a bank that will loan you $180,000 with a $20,000 down payment. So, you begin looking at other options.

You notice that your primary residence (the home you live in most of the time) has $250,000 in equity – the difference between how much the bank thinks your home is worth and how much you have left on your loan.

Now, you find a bank that will give you a HELOC loan at a low interest rate so you can take a loan against the equity you have. Since you have more equity than your investment property's purchase price, you use that equity to finance that new property! Imagine if you paid down that loan while you paid down your original mortgage and then did it again. You could buy an almost unlimited amount of houses with just your original investment!

Another strategy investors use is taking out a HELOC and using that money as a down payment. So, let's say you took out that original $200,000 HELOC and found 20 houses that only needed a $10,000 down payment. I wouldn't advise buying 20 properties because there is such a thing as *growing too fast,* but I hope it demonstrates the power of leveraging your equity.

3. Soft Money Lenders

Investing in real estate has become an entire industry. When the market is up, you can find money almost anywhere because people want to make money on loans. Soft money lenders are one type of these people. Hard money lenders are the other type, but we'll talk about them later.

Soft money lenders are investor-specific loan servicers. Many of them go to local REIA meetings to network with the people with whom they want to loan money. Since they are friendly with investors, they will not be surprised when you tell them you want to buy an investment property.

Soft money lenders are willing to take on more risk than banks. They usually ask for smaller down payments, usually don't check your credit score, and are willing to loan money against a "less-than-attractive" property.

In exchange, they charge a higher interest rate. The interest rates can range from as low as 3.5% to 8%. I've even seen some soft money lenders perform unsecured loans up to $1,00,000! *(That means they don't foreclose on your house if you don't pay them back; they just ruin your credit and your reputation.)* The best part about soft money lenders is that they are willing to lend to an LLC; unlike conventional loans or vacation rental loans.

You can find these lenders on Facebook groups and at your local REIA clubs.

4. Small Business Loan

Another way of financing your Airbnb property is through using a small business loan. Since listing a property on Airbnb has become a business model for many, lenders are now willing to offer small business loans for things like paying down payments on properties, paying for operating expenses, marketing, and other small business needs.

However, these loans are not easy to secure because most lenders will want to see a good track record of how your Airbnb properties have performed over time. New Airbnb hosts won't have this kind of information and may find it difficult to convince lenders that they have a good business model. Qualifying for a small business loan also requires you to be registered as a legal entity and have all of your taxes and paperwork in order.

5. Hard Money Loans

Hard money lenders also try to make money on investment property mortgages. These lenders use short-term loans with nasty high-interest rates and insane payback schedules. Usually, you only use hard money for flips, but some desperate investors try to use them to invest in rentals.

There are "longer term" hard money loans that have a term of about two years and has double-digit interest rates. Then, there are "shorter term" hard money loans that last for a few months. Those are called bridge loans - a short-term, unfavorable loan that you take out because you need money *right now*. Bridge loan terms are probably the worst sort of loan – even when compared with title or payday loans!

Nevertheless, because they have such a quick approval time and don't place as much emphasis on your credit score, many investors who don't qualify for the other types of loans will attempt to use them.

The decision to take out a hard money loan is not one that you, a new investor, should take lightly. Hard money loans are ridiculously costly and should only be used as a temporary solution. Their interest rates are just way too high – it's like buying a house with a credit card.

Location Is Everything!

When shopping for an Airbnb property, very few investors will compromise when finding the best location. Have you heard realtors emphasize that the three most important aspects of real estate are location, *location*, LOCATION? That's because when you purchase just-an-ok property in the right location, you stand to receive an excellent return on your investment.

For Airbnb investing, location is much more essential. Guests rate you on your location and whether or not it lived up to its description on the listing. Guests are attracted to great locations, so you're more likely to get guests if you are in the right location; it's your property's greatest asset.

Think about it. How many people want to travel to the middle of nowhere, Wisconsin? It's not a destination you consider when you think about vacationing. Compare that to Miami . . . and you get the point.

I can't tell you how many times I've been disappointed by an overly-hyped location that turned into a nightmare. It doesn't matter how much you dress up that Wisconsin listing; it's still the middle of nowhere!

This whole line of thinking hails back to the same philosophical question that the realtors-of-old pondered while sipping their mulled coffee in their ancient Starbucks. *What makes for a great location?*

There are a lot of competing answers, but I think I've figured it out. A great location can't be shown; it can only be *felt*. Things like the sense of community, tranquility, safety, access, desirability (is it Instagram-able?), and convenience matters most when you're trying to determine if a location is great or not. It's why I had to fly out to see my first Airbnb. Some things just can't be determined through pictures, at least not for the uninitiated!

Of course, you can't just fly around the world, aimlessly searching for a location . . . well, that sounds pretty fun, but I, for one, don't have the time to do that! I'm on a tight schedule.

There is another way to determine great locations: check to see if other people are making money there. This is a vital part of due diligence – and the subject of the next chapter.

Finding a great location is the single most crucial part of investing; you shouldn't just settle for *any* location. You must dedicate enough time to researching, so don't expect to find the perfect location in a day.

We want to find an area that will reach a specific occupancy all year round, not just 100% in the busy season and 0% the rest of the year. I prefer my STRs (short-term rentals) to have no less than 70% occupancy at any point in the year.

In fact, this is the number one goal when you're trying to buy your first STR: I will buy an STR that will be booked all year round and not merely during busy seasons. If you believe in the law of attraction, add this to your daily mantras.

You should know how busy the area is throughout the year. Find out how crowded it gets during busy seasons and how quiet it is during off-seasons. This approach may seem tedious, but I promise it will pay off. *Location, location, location* means more than a beautiful home.

Here's the brainstorming process that I go through when I think I have a great property lined up. First, I think about all of the things I would do if I stayed at that rental. If I'm looking at a condo in the city, I want to make sure that it is located close to popular landmarks: zoos, museums, cool restaurants, parks, and malls are all excellent activities.

But if I'm looking to purchase a property in a more scenic and relaxing area – say, near a mountain or beach – I'd think about the nearby outdoor activities. How far is the STR from a nearby town? Does it have free transportation there? Are there any hiking trails or scenic views nearby?

I recommend you purchase an Airbnb in an area in which *you* like to vacation. This gives you an advantage when selecting the property because you'll already know what vacationers like there. It will also make writing the listing much easier because you're already in the mind of your potential guest.

Another essential tip to remember when looking for the best location is to visit the property before making a purchase. I remember the moment I realized that I had found "the one." I could hardly contain my excitement!

I knew that looking at the photos online was simply not enough to make me sign on the dotted line. I wanted to see the property (and my other choices) in its raw, UN-photoshopped state and imagine a guest staying a few nights in the home. I needed to see what the geographical landscape was like, the neighborhood "vibe," and what my guests could look forward to.

I wanted to check out the surrounding neighborhood to see if there was any sketchy atmosphere. Live the nightlife. Experience the tourist attractions and see the sights. You need to have this same mindset. Many experienced STR investors have a gut feeling about all of those things; you probably don't... yet! Make sure you get a sense of the neighborhood before you go all in.

Talking to your realtor about the general sentiment around STRs should also be on your list of things to do. They will have their ear to the ground about changes in local laws, town developments, or new regulations. Use the time you have with the realtor to ask as many questions as you need to get the full picture of the location. If you don't love what you hear, you should read between the lines and find a new investment city. Do this before you go; call them first.

All that said, if other Airbnb investors are making money in that area, you will too. Don't try to be a trailblazer and invest in a town that has no other Airbnbs. Think of yourself as a business owner; new business owners often believe the fallacy that you need to be first to be successful. But success in the business world isn't really about having the idea first; it's about having the best advertising.

Being a trailblazer can sometimes lead to success, but often, it doesn't matter. For instance, why are there no SFRs on Mars? It's a silly question with an obvious answer in this case, but I use it to prove a point. When you don't see Airbnbs somewhere, you should ask the question "Why not?" and dig around until you find the answer.

Why aren't there Airbnbs in this city? *Oh, because the regulations make them illegal.*

Why aren't there Airbnbs in this town? *Oh, because there isn't enough demand.*

It's not just enough to be first. You also need to make sure you can be profitable. Often, if you see others doing it successfully, then it's profitable! All you need to do is figure out what you will do to be unique and how to market that uniqueness – especially when you're starting!

TL;DR

STRs are all about *vacationing*, so you need to select a location people prefer for vacations. You can always compromise on your home's aesthetics, but you certainly cannot compromise on the location. Likewise, you can always upgrade your house, but you can't easily upgrade your location. If you cannot find a property in the best location that is within your price, continue your search in other smaller towns or regions.

Try to select towns that you love to vacation in; if you love it, others probably love it too. It will also give you an advantage later when writing your listing.

Regardless of which town you choose, you're sure to make money during the year because there's something about hot beaches and relaxing mountaintops that travelers can't get enough of.

CHAPTER

Six Steps to Purchase the Perfect Property

———

Real estate is an imperishable asset, ever-increasing in value. It is the most solid security that human ingenuity has devised. It is the basis of all security and about the only indestructible security."

~ Russell Sage

What You Can Expect in This Chapter:

- *Two ways to find a great city to invest in*

- *How to perform due diligence so you can be confident you're going to make money*

Now that you have a basic idea of how to finance your rental and what makes a good location, let's talk about finding one!

Step 1: Make a List of Places of Interest

For now, I would like you to pick the ideal location you see your Airbnb situated. Do you see your home surrounded by beaches or mountains?

Here are a few reasons why Airbnb beach and mountain homes are a must-have for newbie property investors.

- Beach towns make a lot of money in the summer and spring. Busy season starts picking up in March and hits its peak in July. People flock to the beaches in the summer, causing the nightly price of Airbnb to go through the roof. Since you will be adjusting your prices all year, you'll make a lot of money in the summer. Beaches are still pretty warm in the winter, too, and some people search for a discounted place to spend the holidays. You'll make money all year with beach towns.

- Mountain towns aren't ghost towns, as many would assume. They are one of the best places travelers visit for winter retreats, ski trips, and some much-needed R&R time in a cozy log cabin. They also serve a two-fold purpose; in the summertime, hikers and other mountain dwellers who want to appreciate the scenic view of mountains and forests look for accommodations.

- Focusing on beach and mountain towns is an excellent option for a first-time investor because these places are popular hot spots for travelers. Since I like to focus on vacation areas, this is the obvious choice.

But in the end, there are no wrong answers here; just start writing down a list of locations that you like visiting. It doesn't even have to be in your own country - it could be anywhere in the world!

If you can't think of any (or only have a few), then I have a solution for you: travel blogs! **Blogs, tv shows, and friends are all great places to find ideas on cities to check out for your first Airbnb investment.**

I prefer blogs when I'm sitting down to search because I only have a few hours each day dedicated to investing; anything I do needs to be *fast*. Talking to friends is nice and watching TV is great, but they're both too distracting if you're trying to be efficient.

Blogs are also a great source of information about what travelers like to see. Read a few travel blogs, and you'll get a pretty good idea of what your guests might want to find when they tour specific locations.

Once you've added a few travel blog locations to your list, we can move on to step 2!

Step 2: Find a City to Invest In

Personally, I love the process of the initial screening because I love money. There's nothing better than sitting down each morning with a hot cup of coffee and daydreaming about how I will #KMJ22 (kill my job by 2022) or #RMF25 (retire my family by 2025). So, screening these locations and discovering how much money I could make is very exciting!

There are two ways you can go about screening: the free, hard way and the paid, easy way. I'll explain how to do both here – just in case!

The Free Way

The free way involves three tools: www.Airdna.co, www.Airbnb.com, and www.Zillow.com (or your country's equivalent).

We'll start our search on www.Airdna.co. This is a cool website that takes information from short-term rental providers like Airbnb and VRBO, aggregating it into an easy-to-understand report. I don't recommend purchasing anything through it because I *hate* the pricing structure, but I do like using their free resources.

Let's say the first city on my list is Anchorage, Alaska. Many people love snow sports and think Alaska is absolutely breathtaking, so why wouldn't it make a good spot for an STR?

Type in Anchorage, Alaska in Airdna's search bar. You should see a screen come up with all kinds of information (and some information blocked out!).

You can use the Market Grade, Average Daily Rate, Occupancy Rate, and Revenue to determine if you think this area will be a good investment. If I'm looking at this, I'm getting pretty excited. The overall occupancy rate seems to be around 70% for the year, the average daily rate isn't too bad, and the revenue looks like it'll work as long as the real estate in the area is pretty cheap.

Now, look at the Active Rentals panel. It seems that most of the rentals here are entire homes, and only a few are for a private room. This makes me interested in private room investments. That revenue figure ($1,372) is pretty low, so we need to find cheap real estate to turn a profit. Renting out by the room is a great strategy (though it does involve a little bit more effort from the cleaning staff). Either way, I'll look at both (by the house and by the room) later.

Let's pause a moment here. Real estate is comparative – going back to our location, location, location discussion last chapter. A beautiful mansion in the middle-of-nowhere, Wisconsin, will be the same price as a one-bedroom flat in the heart of New York City!

With real estate, your property is only worth as much as the same property down the block. Houses don't have inherent value. You can't just look at a 3-bedroom/2-bath and decide that it's worth one dollar. You have to price your house to the market or else you will either 1) leave money on the table or 2) never sell it!

But location isn't the only thing that determines how much a house will be worth. The amount of space, bedrooms, bathrooms, materials (and a whole bunch of other things) factor in as well. I'm sure if you've been investing for a while, you know that the more detailed you can get when you're comparing (or, as the popular kids like to call it *comping*) your house, the better; but if you're new to investing, you're in for a wild ride!

Leave Airdna up and open a new tab. Type in www.Zillow.com. Zillow is an aggregation website that tries to keep track of all the houses that have been bought and sold. It uses publicly available information, so sometimes it can be off. Don't take Zillow as gospel, but realize that it's probably good enough for a cursory look!

Type in the city or zip code. You should see a bunch of houses pop up! Start looking at the prices. Sometimes, if you have an extensive area like Anchorage, you need to niche down a little bit. The best way to do this is to look at Airdna's map and see where there are already some Airbnbs – but not so many that it looks crowded. I also like to check the crime in the area to be sure that there isn't any violent crime. You can do this at https://spotcrime.com/.

Once you've found an area with some Airbnbs that looks safe enough to vacation in, you need to decide what kind of property you want to invest in. I usually start by looking at either condos or townhomes because they tend to be cheaper than a single-family home.

So, to put this all together, I've selected townhomes between Raspberry Rd and Dimond Blvd. As you'll see below, I've narrowed my search in Zillow down to this specific area. *(You might need to select "Townhomes" from the dropdown menu and click "Remove Boundary," and redraw the boundary to get your Zillow to look like mine.)*

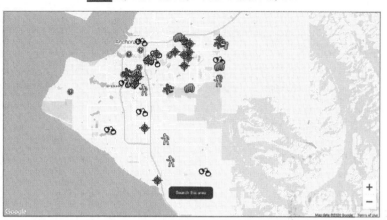

To the right of this map are all of the properties in that area. Right now, there are five townhomes for sale. Two 3/2 (three beds, two baths), two 2/2, and one 1/2. Click on a few of them and look through the pictures. Airbnbs are usually pretty nice, so make sure you select one that looks nice on the inside *and the outside* to compare.

Airdna has a really cool feature that lets you see what each property could potentially earn. Like Zillow, it's an aggregate of other properties in the area, so it might not be accurate to the dollar, but it will get you in the right ballpark.

Go to https://www.airdna.co/vacation-rental-data/app/rentalizer and paste in the address from Zillow. Make sure you select the correct address from the dropdown! The website should reload with a bunch of information about that address. Near the search bar, there should be a dropdown for beds, baths, and guests. Select the correct number of beds and baths. If you'd like, play with the number of guests because it can affect your profit margins.

A quick note on guests. Airbnb lets you select the number of guests that can use your property. The more guests a property can hold, the more you can charge per night. We'll talk more about this later, but this is why it will affect your profit margins!

Now that you have an approximation for how much revenue this particular home will provide, you'll need to estimate your expenses. There are far more expenses to an Airbnb property than just the mortgage. For instance, there's the maid service, the consumables, the utilities, and the yard… you get the picture! So, we just need to estimate these expenses to arrive at a good picture of our area's profits.

If you scroll down, Airdna.co even has a calculator that you can use to calculate your expenses. We'll go over what each of the fields mean and how you can find accurate information to fill them in depth later on.

Go through this same process for all of these homes in this area. The *Done For You Suite* at the beginning of this book includes a spreadsheet called *Airbnb City Comping Spreadsheet*. This will help you keep track of the information you get from Airdna, so make sure you plug it all in as you go!

Once you've finished working on three to five homes in an area of each type, you're pretty much done calculating your revenue; move on to a different area. Again, we still need to calculate the expenses and compare that, but I'll show you how to do that after showing you the fast way to comp.

The Fast Way

You have to admit; the free way is very time-consuming. As I've grown older into my extreme, late 20's, I've come to realize that I only have so much time. So, I tend to favor spending money in lieu of time. If you're like me, then the fast way is going to interest you quite a bit! If you aren't, then at least hear me out!

First, I have to get a little philosophical with you.

If you've heard about the FIRE movement, then you know there are all sorts of people who retire. Some people like to retire as soon as possible on as little money as possible. We call those people *lean FIRE*. They retire on as little as a million dollars! (And I'm not just talking about retirement-aged people, 20 and 30-year-olds do it too!)

Then there are the people who want to live a comfortable retirement life. They take a little longer to retire but generally retire with 3 to 5 million. They are called *fat FIRE*. They still need to look after their expenses, but generally, they should be able to live a very comfortable life for the duration of their retirement. There are also 30-year-olds retiring to the fat FIRE lifestyle – though less than lean FIRE because they must save 3-5 times the amount of money.

Then, there's my favorite group... OBESE FIRE. Obese FIRE retirees try to retire to a life of absolute luxury. Usually, you can't save enough to OBESE FIRE; you must set up streams of income.

That's where I am, baby - setting up my streams of income so I can retire into the lap of luxury. Now, do I think I can do this by 2022? Probably not. 2022 is just the start of my obese FIRE journey. My goal is just to quit my job in 2022. Once I do that, I'll have all day to set up more streams of income instead of just three or four. That's why I'm trying to *kill my job* by 2022 and *retire my family* by 2025. Those three years will be crucial because I will have all day to work on my passive, retirement income.

And that is why I don't mind paying for things that save me time. Because you can always make more money, but you can't buy more time. And I am running out of it!

So, there's my spiel on why I recommend you spend a little extra money to purchase one of the plans in Mashvisor; it will save you *buckets of time*. And if you use my link below, you'll also save a ton of money.

When you go to Mashvisor, you're provided with a choice: a cheap plan, a middle-of-the-road plan, and an expensive plan. While you might get by with the cheap plan, I recommend the middle-of-the-road package. Usually, they give you a 7-day free trial, so if you don't like it (and prefer to finding your STRs gratis), you can always cancel it before the trial ends.

Mashvisor and I have teamed up to give my readers 15% off any plan. At the time of this writing, the lite plan is normally 17 bucks a month. Because you're my reader, you get 15% off that. That works out to roughly three Starbuck coffees (because everyone *loves* to compare their discounts to coffees). Just go to www.AutomatedRetirees.com/links/Mashvisor for your 15% off coupon.

Once you're in, search for your designated town and, once there, you'll see a dropdown in the top left-hand corner. I like to look at the heatmap for "Airbnb Cash on Cash Return" Here's a picture of that same Anchorage map.

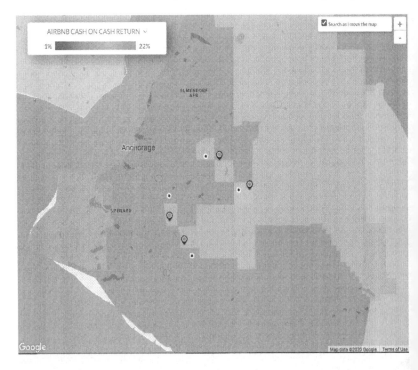

Looking to the top left, you'll see the heat map; immediately, you know that that little area we selected earlier will *not* be a great place to invest! In this case, being in the red means the returns are pretty poor.

Keep in mind that the percent return up there is pretty broad. In this case, the orange area is probably just fine, but the red areas are not even worth a second glance!

Always take a look at the scale before you judge the area because the scale *does* move around. If the max return were only 3%, then the scale would be 1% to 3%. Then again, if the min returns were 8%, then it's an absolute banger of an area… even though it would be red!

With Mashvisor, you can quickly scan an area to see if it looks like a good one, pretty much negating the need for a lot of brainstorming to find little towns that could be profitable. Instead, you can roam around the country of your choice and look for green!

This map is a very impressive feature, but it's just one of many in Mashvisor. (But wait… there's more!) If you look to the right of it, you will see a bunch of properties. You can choose between investment, Airbnb, and traditional. If you'd like to see how many Airbnbs or traditional rentals are in a specific area, you can do it all from this one platform.

The *Investment* tab is the one I look at most often. When I'm looking through Mashvisor, I try to find short-term rentals that net at least an 8% ROI. Of course, that's just where I start. As I said earlier, Mashvisor tries its best to be accurate, but it is usually approximate at best.

As a recap, we use Mashvisor to find an area we think looks good. With just a glance required, it proves to be a lot less work than Airdna's platform.

Step 3: Check the Law

Each city has a different view of Airbnbs. In some cities, it's like the wild, wild west: there's no regulation, no laws, you can just Airbnb it up until the cows come home. However, a lot of the larger, touristy cities around the world are steeped in regulation. Some go so far as to ban short-term rentals altogether. Others choose to discourage STRs by levying a rather hefty (and completely inappropriate, in my opinion) hotel tax. Other cities require you to apply for a license, limiting the number that are issued.

When you choose to invest in an area, you need to ensure that you are compliant with all the local laws and regulations. If you aren't, the city has every right to fine you until you shut down. And sure, while you can probably get away with it for a little while, you won't get away with it forever. They will find you. And they will *fine* you.

There are several ways you can determine if the city you are looking at has a special short-term rental regulation. The first – and best – resource is Airbnb's website. They have a section called "responsible hosting" that stays apprised of laws for many larger cities worldwide. Big cities are where most of the regulation occurs, so they are what Airbnb has focused on. If you invest in a smaller town, you'll need to move on to resource number two: that town's rules and regulations.

Finding the local laws and regulations can take a little bit of internet sleuthing, but it's well worth your time. A few minutes on Google could save you from a $100,000 bad decision! If nothing pops up on Google, you should not assume that there are no regulations.

The next places I look are Facebook and Meetup. Join the groups that look like they are specific to or near the area you're planning on investing in and ask this straightforward question:

Hello! I'm looking to purchase an Airbnb in XXX city, but I'm not from here. Does anyone know what laws and regulations I should be aware of?

The last place I look is the government website. Mostly because *finding* the applicable laws is hard; reading through them is even worse. But when push comes to shove, I find the local Municipality's website and begin scouring the regulations.

You can do any of these in any order if you'd like; that's just the order I prefer. For instance, if you're a lawyer and like reading through laws, maybe the municipality's website is your first stop.

Bottom line: the information you need to get is:

- Is it legal to rent an Airbnb here?

- Are there any regulations?

- Do I need a license?

- Is there a special tax?

All of this information varies by city or county. But once you find a great place to invest, the good news is that you can buy as many houses as you'd like there - you only have to do this search once per new municipality.

Now that you've thoroughly vetted your area, let's find some property!

Step 4: Look for Competition

After that cursory check, it's time to get serious. Let's dig a little deeper into some of these potential investment towns, shall we?

Open up Airbnb.com. Type in one of the zip codes that you're considering and scroll through the Airbnbs. I know this might seem like double work, but we need to do it. We're about one chapter away from actually purchasing an Airbnb (gasp!) If you're like me, that sentence probably made you feel nervous.

Don't worry! That's why we're doing *a lot* of due diligence. Trust me; mistakes will be made on the first, second, and maybe even third short-term rental. But, if we do a lot of thorough research, we'll make fewer mistakes. That said, making mistakes now – early on – is to be accepted and wholeheartedly embraced. You will never actually invest your money if you don't become okay with investing it less than perfectly.

Let's take a pause and talk about a little concept called *failing forward*.

Failing Forward, a book by John C. Maxwell, discusses your failure being what actually should propel you forward. If you grew up in the United States (like me), you might have an unhealthy relationship with failure. Maybe you think that making mistakes and failing are bad things. I know I used to! But this couldn't be further from the truth.

The only way that people learn is by making mistakes. That goes double for hard-headed entrepreneurs like us! If you try to do everything perfectly the first time, you're probably never even going to start because you're too worried about messing up. If you never start, you never succeed. And that's a failure in and of itself.

Why do I mention <u>Failing Forward</u>? Well, when you first start a business, the stakes are not that high. While they probably *feel* high, they aren't nearly as high as when you've gone *all-in.* For instance, if you make a mistake now when you have one STR, that just affects your one STR. If you make a mistake later when you have 10 or 20 STRs, that mistake affects them *all*!

So, it's actually in your best interest to make all of your mistakes now, in the beginning. Not only do you avoid making much more costly mistakes later on, but you also gain more knowledge that carries through to your business later. Also, realizing that you're going to make a mistake or two (and it likely won't be that bad) will help you get started.

Did you know that most real estate investors fail because they never even start? Don't let that be you! Of course, we're not just going to dive in without thinking; we're going to try to avoid making as many mistakes as possible. After all, why else did you pick up this book?

Bottom line: don't let the possibility of the unknown stop you from creating the life you want.

If you have a problem with failure, I highly recommend you purchase a copy of *Failing Forward*. It's a great book that you can buy here: www.AutomatedRetirees.com/recs/failingforward.

With that out of the way, let's get back to www.Airbnb.com. We want to look at our potential competition and size them up. To do this, just put in your prospective investment city (leave everything else blank) and click the magnifying glass.

First off, make sure there are active Airbnb listings. If there aren't many active Airbnb listings, you proceed with caution because it means that this area probably isn't profitable. Not always, but certainly more often than not.

Next, glance through all of the pictures, looking for trends. Are they all downtown? Are they all farm-like? Do people show the outside of their house or primarily a room?

Now, look at the cancelation policy. If we were super picky, we'd want to pick an area that predominately has a moderate or strict policy. If everyone is flexible, you'll probably be forced to have a flexible policy, or else you won't be able to compete.

Another metric to consider closely is overall ratings. Most Airbnbs have very close to – if not exactly – 5 stars. That isn't a problem, but it will be easier for you to shoot to the top of the search algorithm if other homes don't have a 5-star average and you *do*.

Make a note of the average daily rate, the number of rooms, and what types of properties are popular here. You want to set yourself apart, so if you see that most houses around the area have two beds, you want to have three.

Also, consider what kind of amenities the rentals have and start thinking of ways to make your rental more convenient and comfortable for your guests.

You can see a lot of this information on Mashvisor if you look for it. Mashvisor even provides a nifty comp guide; by all means, use that too! But always consult with the Airbnb because it has the freshest and most accurate information. When making sure you're investing in a great area, it's always best to double-check with *the source* before you make a decision.

Who knows? A law might have recently changed causing all of the STRs to shut down. This would only be reflected on Airbnb because Mashvisor is an aggregation. That means it will need some time to catch up. I.e. it's not fresh.

Step 5: Compare Home Prices

Now that you know what type of house you'd like to buy (location, rooms, nearby attractions, amenities, etc.), begin looking at the price of houses that fit your criteria. I like using house aggregation websites like http://www.zillow.com and http://www.realtor.com for quick price comparisons.

If you bought Mashvisor, this might seem silly - but it's not! You don't just want to see what you can buy houses for now; you want to get a *base price* for the area. Compare prices predicated on the following:

- What type of property is it? Are you purchasing a condo or a house?

- What size is the property?

- How much do you think you can make from this property monthly and yearly?

- Does it have excellent profit potential?

- Is the location of the property easy to access? Can your guests easily get around without having to sit in heavy traffic or wait hours for transportation?

- What's the competition like in the area? How many other short-term rentals are there?

- Will your home have enough character to stand out?

- What will it cost you to maintain your property?

- Have you considered the monthly expenses, unforeseen repairs, insurance, taxes, and mortgage repayments?

- Are you planning on hiring a property manager to handle the operations, or will you do it yourself? (You would still need to pay Airbnb a 3% flat fee for every guest you host.)

Now that you have taken a cursory glance at the area, all you have to do is take what you would spend on the house (mortgage, your estimated amenities and property management fees, taxes, etc.) and compare it to what you would earn. The next chapter goes over this in depth. Right now, we are just trying to find our niche.

Make sure that these houses or condos can be bought for around $100,000. Remember, we want to leverage our money any way we can. If you get lucky enough to find some tiny town with tiny homes for sale, you might even get a better deal!

Step 6: Separate Yourself From the Competition

Chances are high that there will already be a few Airbnb homes in your prospective investment town. This isn't a bad thing. Healthy competition can serve to boost the number of tourists coming to town and even promote more economic activity in the area (this is good news for you, my friend).

However, it is still crucial that you stand out from the rest, making your home or condo feel like one-of-a-kind. Make sure that, at the very least, you have all of the amenities that your competitors have. It's even better if you have more – more rooms, a more spacious sitting area, or more modern finishes (if that's the look you're going for) can convince prospective guests to stay with you over someone else.

The one thing I recommend you shy away from is water, at least for your first property. Pools and hot tubs will set you apart, but they are also a liability. You can be sued if someone gets hurt or drowns, and I doubt you'll have the proper business structure to weather that. If you want to ignore this advice, make sure you hire a real estate specific lawyer to set your business structure up *correctly*. And listen carefully to their advice about bank accounts, spending, and piercing the corporate veil.

Look at top properties to see your competition. Write down the amenities they have and consider how modern their interiors are. The whole point of assessing your competition is to know what type of property you need to buy. By now, the end of this chapter, you should have a clear idea of what niche(s) you want to invest in and in which town(s).

TL;DR

You can also use various online tools like Mashvisor to help you search for and find the perfect location in a matter of minutes.

Once you know *where* you want to invest, you'll need to narrow down what you'd like to invest *in*. The best way to do this is with a competition analysis on your future rivalry. Are there any holes in the market? If so, fill those holes!

Now that we've picked a few ideal locations and know what kind of house we want to buy, let's look at some contenders!

CHAPTER

The Perfect Purchase... And Your Contingency Plan!

_____

"Buying real estate is not only the best way, the quickest way, the safest way, but the only way to become wealthy."

~ Marshall Field

What You Can Expect in This Chapter:

- *A few key pointers that make the process much smoother; I know from firsthand experience how stressful it is to get all your ducks in a row before starting.*

- *Three questions that you need to answer honestly. I'll break them down and leave you with some food for thought.*

- *A list of must-have items to buy for your Airbnb home. Shopping can be a nightmare for some people, but a well-organized list can put your anxiety to rest.*

Baby Steps

After 62 long days (yes, I counted), the bank finally closed on my first property. Nothing can describe the sheer amount of relief—then sudden terror—I felt as I signed the contract. Sure, the price of the house was supposed only to be $600 per month...

Of course, my mind immediately started thinking glass half empty. What if something went wrong? What if I miscalculated? What if Mashvisor lied and I didn't make that much? What if a hurricane came and destroyed my entire investment? What if no guest ever came to stay? Was it even worth it to invest out here? What if...

But the ink was dry.

My dad is an expert interior designer, so I immediately enlisted his help. I am a great analytical thinker but when it comes to interior design... let's just say I'd rather hire out!

I had applied for a 0% APR credit card around the same time I had applied for a mortgage. The plan was to use my father's design know-how and some free money to buy the furniture (and earn some points along the way).

We hit up Sam's Club for some cheap bed frames, mattresses, and pillows. The rest of the furniture was bought from Walmart, Target, Ikea, and all

68

the consignment stores we could find. In the end, we furnished that entire 3-bedroom/2-bathroom home for $3,000. And dang, did it look amazing!

Once it was furnished, I nervously shot a million pictures with my phone. Now, I'm not a photographer, but years browsing through Pinterest will teach you a thing or two. After a few rounds of editing and sharpening the lighting, they came out pretty good.

We were well on our way to making this thing work!

Are You Sure This Is What You Want?

I won't sit here and tell you that purchasing your first Airbnb will be a walk in the park. Any new skill is intimidating, especially when you're throwing around tens of thousands of dollars! But, like any skill, it's all just a learning process. As long as you keep on going, you will succeed. You just have to push through!

In the end, Airbnbs are easier than other real estate investments – definitely not as hard as flipping, managing long-term rentals, or wholesaling (believe me!) All things considered, Airbnb has a much smaller learning curve and is pretty forgiving.

Starting new things is hard – especially businesses! I know there were many times in my journey that I felt like giving up but didn't because I made sure to have *an anchor* who would pull me back from the edge. You should consider finding your own anchor for those moments where you just feel like giving up.

Find someone that has the following three traits:

- You trust them implicitly. You would tell them your deepest, darkest secret and know they wouldn't tell anyone else. You need *that kind of trust.*

- They love you.

- They always give it to you straight, whether it's a tag sticking out of the back of your shirt to keeping you accountable for your goals, they tell you.

Explain your plan to them and ask them to hold you accountable. Be careful who you pick because secret trait number four is:

- They cannot be a Debbie Downer!

Choose someone who has faith that you can do "it," whatever "it" is. Someone who will encourage you when you try to chicken out. We're going to call this person your anchor because they're going to tether you to this idea. And once you get going, they won't let you wiggle your way out of it.

For me, this person is always my mother. Gentle as a lamb but as fierce as a tiger when she needs to be! She is always positive, steady as a rock, and *never* lets me wiggle out of my goals. Find someone that will be gentle but firm with you.

In fact, when I had this crazy idea of retiring in 2025, she was the first person I told. I'm a little ashamed to say this, but I didn't think she'd go for the idea. I thought she'd laugh at me for even daring to dream something as crazy as that… but she didn't. She felt that if I *said* I was going to do it, I *was* going to do it.

From that day on, she's been my sounding board, my rock, my light in the darkness. When you have a goal as big as mine (and I'm sure you do), you sometimes need a kick in the pants. She's my designated kicker. Make sure you find yours!

That reminds me. Before we talk about *how* to comp an STR, let's make sure that you are in the right mindset for investing.

Two Questions That Every Airbnb Investor Needs to Answer

Yes, I know… I've buried this deep within the book. After all, if you've read past the first three chapters and halfway through the fourth of a five-chapter book, you're probably dead set on investing! But now, you know a great deal more about Airbnbs, and you have all the background information you need to answer these questions intelligently and honestly.

There are three crucial things you need to be sure of before we continue here. These questions will shape the kind of experience you are looking for as an investor and help you figure out whether you can afford to start investing *right now*. Take your time with this section. Grab a coffee and go to a quiet place. Put the book down in between each question and really think about it.

How Passive Do You Want this Business?

There are no formal rules about how involved you need to be as a host. Some hosts *love* to meet new people and deeply enjoy the customer-interaction aspect of this business.

They'll spend their time personally greeting their guests, driving them around town, feeding them, etc. This type of person usually just has one Airbnb property, and typically it's their own house! They do Airbnb to meet new people *with the added income as a cherry on top*! If that's you, then, *GO, YOU!* It's not very scalable, but nothing is stopping you!

Other hosts don't even live in the same town as their Airbnb property, merely giving their guests a passcode to a lockbox and a book to guide them on their stay. They still text or email their guests and do a lot of the customer service required with Airbnb, *but that's about it*. If you don't want to hire a property manager, but you still want to scale your business, this is the type of host you need to be. Distant, cordial, and raking in that dough!

The third type: a host who doesn't want to deal with *anything*, outsourcing *all* the work to a property manager. That said, with all of the automation built around Airbnb, you're able to outsource most of the work to robots! I'm writing a book specifically about this topic now. If you downloaded my *Done For You Suite*, I'll send you an email when it's released!

Automating the business end costs you close to nothing . . . at least when you compare it to the property manager's fee. Property managers charge anywhere between 10% to 35% of your monthly earnings, but they are responsible for taking care of your guests, optimizing your listing, and even coordinating your cleaning and maintenance crews.

While automation handles most of that work for you, you'll still have to spend a few hours a week checking in on your properties to ensure they are okay.

So, that begs the question . . . what level of involvement do you want to have in your business? There are pros and cons for each, but it comes down to how much time versus money do you have?

If you're a full-time host, you get to micromanage your guests' experience and can handle issues immediately. However, the biggest con in that approach – and what *kills it* for me – is that it's incredibly time-consuming. You will be with your guest most days, cooking for them, cleaning up after them . . . you've temporarily adopted a child!

What's even worse is some guests don't like this kind of attention; they just want to be left alone to explore a new place. In my opinion, this squarely represents diminishing returns – especially if your goal is to set up a passive stream of income. As I mentioned earlier, it's not scalable. You'll probably only be able to have two or three properties if you want to be a full-time host. And they'll probably have to be in the city that you live; that significantly limits your options.

The second type of host is the sweet spot, and where I would recommend you begin your Airbnb hosting adventure. You will be responsible for everything like setting up your listing, texting your guests, and organizing your cleaning crew. Most of this can be automated for almost no extra charge. My advice is to manage your first home entirely on your own for a few months. That way you can decide if you can get by with automation. (Usually, you can!) If you still want to hire a property manager, you'll have a better sense of how good job they're doing. The best way to determine if someone is taking advantage of you is to *know* what you're talking about. And the only way to do that is to . . . well, actually *do the work first.*

Last, we have the host that hires a property manager. If you spend a lot of money, you'll have a great one that takes care of your property as if it were theirs. That leaves your time open for other things – like finding more Airbnbs! Property management companies also have set technological systems and processes that make the entire process streamlined.

One con to this approach is that these managers come with a pretty steep price tag. Some property management companies can charge you as much as 35% of your income each month! If you don't try to find an Airbnb that can support this sort of expense from the beginning, then you're probably out of luck.

Another con: if you've never owned a business before, you may not even know if you're a "go with the flow" or an "*I AM the flow*" kind of business owner.

When I started investing and writing, I realized that I was more of the latter. That can seriously get in the way of outsourcing because you feel like no one can do it better than you. And it's true; no one *will!* And if they can, they're probably out of my price range.

If you're like me and you can't just let go and let the property manager do their thing, you might have difficulty hiring this job out. If that's the case, you should probably just stick with automation.

How Do You Feel about Debt?

For the debt lovers...

If you like to (or have to) take out a bunch of high-interest rate credit cards, this section is for you. This book is about investing in real estate, but my overall message is not! My crucial message is about retiring *very comfortably as quickly as possible*. Others - trying only to sell you a real estate investing program – will tell you all kinds of lies.

Oh! You have $100,000 in student loan or personal debt at an 8% interest rate? Well, investing is perfect for you!

No! That's not true.

Debt isn't inherently bad. After all, real estate debt is what allows the average Joe to invest in real estate. Not all of us have $200,000 lying around to buy a house! However, like any other tool, it can be abused.

Getting a stellar college education that sets you up for a great career is an excellent use of debt. Spending that same amount of money on a car... well, that's a terrible use of debt! Racking up $30,000 in credit card debt? Even more terrible!

If you have any debt with an interest rate above 5%, get rid of it before you start investing. I mean it; do not invest in real estate, do not invest in the stock market . . . Heck, don't even save beyond the bare minimum you need for emergencies!

The one exception is if your mortgage rate is above 5%. With your mortgage, you either need to refinance or rent a few rooms out to cover the difference. You might even consider selling! Anything above 5% is an expensive interest rate. If it's real estate and you take 30 years to pay it off, you will have paid almost double the loan amount.

Mortgage amount		Monthly Payments
$ 165,000		$ **885.76**
Mortgage term in years		
30		Total Principal Paid — $165,000
Or		Total Interest Paid — $153,872.04
Term in months		
360		
Interest rate per year		TODAY'S RATES
5 %	CALCULATE	Show amortization schedule

ADD EXTRA PAYMENTS ⌄

From bankrate.com. Compare the red box on the left to the red box on the right.

Sure, try to reason with me. *I needed to rack up this debt because I needed that stuff! It was an emergency!* I'm certainly not the person to tell you not to get the things you want. After all, this book is about retiring wealthy! The mindset of obese FIRE is not the same mindset at lean FIRE where saving up $200,000 and living with your parents on a budget of $1,000 a month (hyperbole – but just barely) is the goal and debt is *abhorred always*. Obese FIRE isn't about sacrificing all joy so you can be a millionaire in ten years!

My message is about setting up the life that YOU want and dream about while making the fewest sacrifices possible to get there. Depreciating assets are false assets (they move in the opposite direction of how true assets move). They do not contribute to your total wealth, and they're likely losing you money each year. Do everything you can to avoid depreciating assets like cars, credit card debt, and other unnecessary purchases.

Debt for appreciating assets is *good debt*. It's debt that makes you money. Like real estate, Airbnbs are considered appreciating assets. Their value will (usually) grow over time – all while they're making money for you! Don't be afraid of this type of debt. But, like my above example be aware of the affects of interest rates!

Some of you may feel cheated because you picked up this book, thinking it would solve your debt issue. You might even try to invest anyway! But if you do that, you're only making things harder on yourself.

First of all, the more debt you have, the harder it will be to get a real estate loan. Banks like to look at how much personal debt you have to determine if you are trustworthy. They call it debt-to-income ratio. A lot of other factors go into their trustworthiness index, but this is a major one! Some banks might not even loan to you if your debt-to-income ratio is too high.

Second, on the off chance that you aren't able to make ends meet with your real estate investment . . . now what? Which do you pay - your credit card or your investment? It's an added risk that you just don't need.

Third, the longer you take to pay off these high-interest rate loans, the more they cost. I am 100% on board with taking out 0% APR credit cards and getting them paid back before the actual interest rate kicks in because that's – in essence - a free loan. But that's a far cry from taking out an 18% APR credit card and never paying it off. You will go bankrupt! It's insane! An 18% APR credit card compounds daily and will almost surely grow faster than you can pay it off.

Not to worry, though. If you have this sort of debt, I'll give you some quick advice on how to pay it off. *These steps are by no means comprehensive, but they are enough to get you started.*

PRE-Step: Make sure you get your spending habits under control. You might have to move into a smaller apartment or back to your folks' home. In the extreme worst case, you might even need to do like Brandon Turner (of Bigger Pockets fame) and rent out your room while you sleep on the couch. Whatever it is, you need to lower your expenses so that you are living below your means. You need to create a reasonable budget – and stick to it. While you're getting that under control . . .

Step 1: Try to refinance. Refinancing isn't just for houses; you can refinance any type of debt! All you have to do is find a bank, credit union, or friend that will take on the debt for you for a lower interest rate. If you have a lot of high-interest credit card debt and a mortgage, your bank will sometimes let you roll that debt into your mortgage. The benefit of that is that the interest rate will go down to a reasonable amount. The downside is that now you just added more debt to a very long-term loan.

Step 2: Start a side hustle. While it might not be time to start investing in a passive income stream, you can still start a second income stream. I mentioned two earlier in this book (renting out rooms in your own home or rental arbitraging someone else's), but there are literally a million more. Find one that you can stand and do it!

I plan on writing a lot of books on this topic, so if it's a few years past 2021, then go check them out! And yes, once you've paid off your debt, come back and buy some Airbnbs.

For the debt haters...

Continuing our conversation from the previous section . . . are you okay with debt? Yes, I know, I just went on a rant about paying down all your personal debts, and now I'm asking if you're okay with debt. But – seriously! There are two ends to every spectrum, and some people don't mind debt . . . other people hate it!

If you hate debt and feel like you want to pay for every property with cash, let me at least try to convince you otherwise.

Many people assume that just because they have enough money stashed in the bank to buy a property in cash, it's the best way to go. If it indeed were the best way to go, don't you think multi-millionaires would buy their Ferraris in cash instead of leasing them?

The secret to being wealthy and reaching our goal of OBESE FIRE, is to leverage debt. Use it as a tool. Borrowing works out in your favor when you can borrow money at a much lower interest rate than you can earn on the money you invest.

In fact, when this is the case, it becomes *profitable* to borrow cash. If you listen to financial gurus like Dave Ramsey, you know how they make it seem like all debt is bad. That's just not true! Some debt is good. There's a big difference between appreciating and depreciating assets. In simple terms, if your asset is depreciating (like most cars, boats, or that stash of the first 150 Pokémon cards you or your kid has buried in the closet), it will not make you money; we can classify it as bad debt.

Let's consider an example: Let's say that you have $100,000 that you'd like to invest. Maybe you threw it in the stock market, but you're looking to diversify

77

your portfolio. Maybe you just stuffed it under your mattress. Whatever the case, you are ready to buy some Airbnbs!

You could just find one Airbnb that costs $100,000 in total. Let's say you do, and it gives you an average return of $1500/month. After one year, you will have $18000! Not bad, but it's far from enough to buy another house *in cash*. For that, you'll have to wait another *5.5 years*!

So, you wait 5.5 years, and you buy another house. Now your total return is $3,000 per month. That's $36,000 per year! So, assuming you can still find a house for $100,000 after waiting this long, you will buy another house in about three more years.

After eight years, you have three houses, each making you about $1,500 per month. If you go on like this, you will be able to buy another house in two years. After roughly ten years, you'll be making $6000/month – or $72,000 per year.

That doesn't sound too bad! But let's look at what would happen if you leveraged your money instead.

Let's start with that same $100,000. This time, we'll say you invested a 20% down payment into five $100,000 houses. Now you have five houses, each making about $1000 per month (it's $500 less per house because your mortgage for each is $500.)

At this point, you're making $5,000 each month. If you wanted to keep going in this fashion, you'd just have to wait four months before you could buy another house for the same price – with a $20K down payment.

Let's look at a chart that assumes you buy a house as soon as you can for a 20% down payment.

Time in Months	Money saved	Monthly Profit	Houses Owned
1	0	5,000	5
2	5,000	5,000	5
3	10,000	5,000	5
4	15,000	5,000	5
5	0	6,000	6
6	6,000	6,000	6
7	12,000	6,000	6
8	18,000	6,000	6
9	2,000	7,000	7
10	9,000	7,000	7
11	16,000	7,000	7

A closer look shows us that in the first month, you buy your five Airbnbs. They each make you $1000. *(I keep the exercise simple by assuming that each Airbnb is listed on the first of the month, bringing you a full month's profit.)* The "Monthly Profit" column shows you this.

Month 2: On the first day of this month, you've made $5000, but it's not enough to put a $20K down payment on another Airbnb, so you let it sit in your checking account while you rack up another month's profits ($5000).

Month 3: At the beginning of this month, you've saved $10,000, halfway to another $20K down payment for your next property!

Month 4: Still owning five properties, you have now saved $15,000.

Month 5: The previous month sees you saving enough for another down payment, so you purchase your sixth property, bringing monthly profits to $6,000 per month.

Month 6: You've got $6,000 in your account; saving towards another down payment!

Month 7: More than halfway to another down payment already!

Month 8: Almost there. You have $18,000 in your account and almost ready to buy your SEVENTH property!

Month 9: Great! You've purchased your seventh property and have $2000 left from that down payment.

Month 10: Already, you've saved nearly half of what you need for your next down payment! Your savings shows $9,000, and you're profits are $7,000 per month!

Month 11: You have $16,000 in your account towards the next property, you own seven Airbnbs making $7,000 per month, and you're poised to buy another property!

You could own eight Airbnb within a year! Leveraging your money helps you grow *much* faster than just spending it all on one house. Borrowing helps you achieve your dreams of #KMJ or #RMF much faster – if you take the leap!

Some realists out there are thinking: *Yeah, but what happens if the profits change? What happens if you can't rent out your house? How do you pay for it then? You're just screwed if you can't rent out eight houses!*

This was meant as an example to show how leveraging works. Owning eight Airbnbs in a year versus five in ten years demonstrates the power of debt. Heads up: you are *really* going to enjoy the next section.

Overleveraging

It just wouldn't be responsible if I didn't caution you about taking on too much debt. That's why I have a few rules that I like to follow.

For instance, each Airbnb that I own has its own $5,000 reserve - in case something disastrous happens. This can be in the form of a 0% APR credit card at first, but you should strive to save it in cold hard cash eventually.

Why? Things break, areas flood, Airbnb changes their algorithm, and you don't realize it in time. Bad stuff happens all the time! Still, you can protect yourself by always keeping some money in reserve – it's the reason why so many Airbnb owners were able to keep their Airbnbs afloat during the COVID-19 pandemic.

$5000 is my go-to because it provides between five to six months of expenses. If you're planning on investing in more expensive Airbnbs, you should definitely have more reserve.

Another rule: I prefer having no more than five loans at a time. Yes, I know .. . I just went through that whole exercise to show you how you could get *eight* Airbnbs in one year – but it was just an exercise in logic! Being overleveraged is worse than being underleveraged because of its risk. If you can't pay your loans back, banks will foreclose on your properties. No one wants that because you lose all the money you put into the loan. Even if you paid $99,000 back from a $100,000 loan, if the bank forecloses on you, you've just lost that $99,000 – plus interest.

The amount of leverage that you can handle is entirely dependent upon your risk tolerance. If you're okay with debts of $800,000 while making $8,000 per month, then more power to you! I'm more averse to that kind of risk – and there's nothing wrong with that.

Similarly, if your risk tolerance tells you to buy one Airbnb at a time, don't let me stop you! I want you to go into this business with your eyes wide open. Yes, it'll take longer to reach your financial goals, but that's not all that life is about. Stress is also a factor; if having high debt stresses you out, by all means, ***avoid it!***

Now that you've answered those questions, let's learn how to do the fun part: comping!

Comping Your First Airbnb

Comping is a term used by real estate professionals as a sort of shorthand for comparing properties. The concept is simple: look at a house you want to buy and compare it with homes in the surrounding area.

When making a real estate investment, there are two sides to consider:

1) What will that property pay you? I.e., how much money are you going to make?

2) How much will this property cost?

For an Airbnb to be a good investment, we need to make sure the property costs less than it pays. To do this, add up all the expenses and subtract them from the profits.

Expenses

Property Tax

Mashvisor tries to keep track of the property taxes. However, Zillow does as well – scroll down to the bottom. These numbers should be enough for your purposes now, but if you want more detail, most cities in the US have all of their property information online. A simple search of XXX county CAD will provide links to that county's appraisal district. *Other countries may have this information online as well.*

Personal/Business Tax

Whatever business structure you choose, taxes must be paid. If you are using a sole proprietor LLC, you will pay two taxes: income tax based on your tax bracket (it changes every year, so google "Tax Bracket" to confirm yours) and self-employment taxes. SE taxes go towards Medicare and social security. As of this writing, self-employment tax is 15.3%. You'll pay both of these taxes on whatever income your property generates. There is some tax magic you can do to lower your burden, but we'll save that discussion for your CPA!

If you are investing through a corporation, your taxes are a lot more complicated. I highly recommend you find a real estate focused CPA and ask that they do your taxes. Generally, corporations are overkill for your first few Airbnbs anyway, so you'll likely have an LLC if you choose to create a business structure.

Lodging Tax

Some cities charge a hotel/lodging tax. Usually, Airbnb automatically withholds this tax for you. You can check to see if your city is on that list here:

https://www.airbnb.com/help/article/1036/how-does-occupancy-tax-collection-and-remittance-by-airbnb-work

Not all cities have a lodging tax, so do your research!

Maintenance

In addition to the $5,000 slush fund, I also like to save 5% of my monthly rent. My husband and I like to call this the *Oh Sh!t Fund* because typically, you only need it when the *sh!t hits the fan!*

Why do I keep the 5,000 reserve AND the extra 5% of every month's rent? Since this is a real asset, something will happen to it. The roof will get damaged, a pipe will burst, a rat can chew through your wires... These are all worst case scenarios but something can and will happen. And it won't always be the tenant's fault. If you have money in reserve, it will be much less stressful to deal with.

If you chose to use a 0% APR credit card for your reserve, then you might want to use a little more of the rent to save up your $5,000 in reserve in hard cash before you save for another one.

Insurance

You can find insurance in several ways. In general, I allow $150 per house per month. However, if you're trying to buy a house in an area with heavy flooding or natural disasters, the insurance costs go up – sometimes drastically. If you aren't familiar with the area, go to any major insurance provider's website and plug in the address. Yes, you'll get some annoying calls, but you'll have a pretty accurate representation of what insurance will cost for that property.

Utilities

Utilities are another one that is hard to estimate for an area in which you're unfamiliar. The good news is most realtors have an approximation of utilities. We aren't ready to call them yet; for now, budget for $500 per month. *Sometimes you just need to fudge it a little so that you can move forward.*

Consumables

This is everything from shampoo to milk. Anything that your guest would get at a hotel is what you'll have at your Airbnb. The amount you budget depends on what you'd like to include; $200 per month is more than generous.

Cleaning

You will need to get your Airbnb cleaned after each visitor. Typically, you pass this expense along to the customer; you can be pretty confident that this expense will be $0 for you.

HOA fees

Zillow includes a decent estimation of the HOA fees. It would be best to ask your realtor for the HOA documents when you start seriously considering a property. You'll have to! Some HOAs don't allow STRs; you must research to determine if you can even buy there.

If you see active Airbnbs in that neighborhood, there's a pretty good chance the HOA allows it. But some people try to skirt the rules, so it never hurts to double-check.

HOA fees are usually between $35 and $150 per month for houses and $350 and $500 for condos. It's very neighborhood-specific so you will need to research this for each property.

Mortgage

Since you're probably going to take out a mortgage, you'll have to pay it! If you choose to invest less than 20% in down payments, you'll also have to pay mortgage insurance. When you get preapproved, your loan servicing company will lock you into a specific interest rate. With that interest rate, you can calculate any mortgage. The Airdna.co and Mashvisor online calculators allow you to input all that information, so don't worry about knowing how to do mortgage math. All you need to know is the interest rate and the purchase price.

The key component to figuring out your mortgage is finding out what a house in the area costs. You can look at homes for sale and do manual calculations if you'd like, but a much faster way is to decide how much you are willing to spend and then set a filter so that you can only spend that much.

To find out how much we can afford, we must get a decent handle on how much we can make. So, let's talk about . . .

Income

Your income will be based on two factors: occupancy and nightly rate. You can estimate this by looking at similar Airbnbs in your area. But this is just an estimation. Your income will be slightly different based on several factors like: How good is your listing? What is your star rating? What is your pricing strategy? We'll go over all of these things in the next chapter. For now, use the comps you get from the surrounding properties for a very good estimation.

When comping, it is advantageous to look for as much accurate, pertinent information as possible. Right now, we have three major tools that we can use: Airbnb.com, Airdna.co, and Mashvisor.

If you have Mashvisor, it will automatically comp out a property for you based on the information you put in. Airdna.co will also do this. This type of investing is relatively easy because many online tools do much of the work for you. Once you have all of the expenses laid out, you only have to plug it into the calculator to see what you're going to spend.

Calculate

Even though I have Mashvisor, I like to use Airdna's calculator as well. The more data I have, the happier I am. Go to Airdna/Invest/Rentalizer. It's free!

Search for the address, then scroll down. You should be able to select "More Details" on the calculator. Enter what we just found and see what kind of return that property will bring you!

Since we are buying these houses using market prices, we don't need to perform a comp on the *actual* sales price. If it's a buyer's market, you can try to get a little bit of a discount. If it's a seller's market, you'll probably pay full price.

Repeat this process with the Airdna or Mashvisor calculator until you find a few houses that you're drawn to. Then, it's time to call up a realtor to schedule a tour. If you can't make it in person, at least request a virtual tour. Different from in-person, but they're better than nothing.

How to Find a Real Estate Agent

Not all realtors are created equal. Some absolutely hate investors! Some are happy to work with them. You need to make an effort to find a real estate agent who at least understands what you're trying to do. Even better if they approve.

Using Zillow, you can find real estate agents – look for them next to any listing. An even better place to find realtors is the Airbnb-specific groups on Facebook or the real estate-specific groups on Meetup.

Most people don't know this, but Meetup has a forum section to ask questions. If you join the Real Estate Investors Association Club for your investment city, you can ask all sorts of questions on the forum. Including…*You guys know an investor-friendly realtor?*

Agents can only offer their services for specific zip codes, so you'll need to find a good agent for each city in which you'd like to invest. Once you do, ask them to set you up on the MLS with emails for properties within your search criteria. Your search criteria should cover the market holes (where it's lacking in meeting specific needs - see the last chapter), like a 2-bedroom/2-bath condo in the city.

Do not try to work with more than one realtor in a city at a time. Realtors get paid by commission, so just make it simple for yourself and stick with one.

Remember to Get Preapproved

We talked about this a little earlier, but this is a great time to get preapproved by a lender. It helps you set your budget and allows you to have a speedy turnaround when you do end up selecting a home. Just make sure that the lender you select services your desired investment area.

In the US, there are both nationwide and local lenders. If you're trying to use local, use lenders within or around your investment city. Most documents can be signed online or remotely anyway.

In fact, in my most recent refinance, I did everything from home. We filled out all the preliminary paperwork online and then used a traveling notary for documents that needed to be notarized. Any lender you use should schedule all this for you, so make sure they offer remote signings before choosing to use them.

Is Your Airbnb Property Legal?

Get the Necessary Permits and Licenses

Some cities ask you to apply for permits and a business license before you list your property. You may be asked to submit documents for each property this is probably the only heavy paperwork you will do before you begin renting out your place). Remember, Facebook or Meetup groups are a great place to figure this out if it isn't called out on Airbnb's website for your city.

You can find the cities here: https://www.airbnb.com/help/topic/272/responsible-hosting. Just navigate to your country and search by city.

You can also consult a local lawyer for a small fee.

Check the Tax Rules in Your Area

Sometimes, Airbnb collects taxes for you – but not all the time. Usually, you can hire a CPA (try Thumbtack) to take care of your personal and business taxes for less than $600. I would strongly recommend this!

In your job description, be sure to say you are trying to invest in Airbnbs; you need to find a CPA specializing in real estate tax because there are unique benefits and advantages. A CPA unfamiliar with real estate may not know about them.

Make Sure Your Property Complies With Safety and Insurance Regulations

Once you have received the green light to start your Airbnb business, you need to make sure that the home meets local building and housing standards. In some cities, a treehouse is a novel and *awesome* investment! In others, you'll get fined or even jailed because you're breaking the law.

From our earlier competitor analysis, you should have an idea of what sorts of properties are available in your area. If you're still not convinced – and you want to rent out a novel property – then you must do some digging into the local laws. If you're planning on renting out a house, duplex, or tiny home, you're probably okay. My warnings apply only if you're trying to rent out an Igloo, a treehouse, or some other crazy structure!

Most states have their laws (property statutes) online. These require certain safety features like up-to-date plumbing, smoke detectors, and non-lead paint. I like to focus on homes built within the last 10 to 20 years, so they are usually up to code. But, if you're worried, you can ask your realtor where to find these safety regulations.

Setting Up Your LLC Online...It's Cheap and Easy!

I'm not a lawyer, but here is my advice: Your Airbnb houses should each have their own LLC. Why? Because if you do get sued, you can simply dissolve the LLC while protecting all of your other assets. (Also, buy rental insurance.)

LLC stands for **L**imited **L**iability **C**ompany. Most are pass-through companies designed to protect you from being liable if something happens within your business asset. For instance, if a guest trips, falls, and breaks their arm – they can sue you.

These suits are pretty rare, but they do happen. That's why most investors protect themselves by putting each asset in its own LLC. These LLCs are then owned by a corporation which, in turn, is owned by another LLC. Talk to a lawyer to set yourself up the right way and learn all your rights.

You don't really need that complicated of a structure when you start out. If you just want to bootstrap your way to $10k, the minimum you should consider is opening an LLC for your first property. The good news is you won't have to become a master at paperwork!

ZenBusiness is one of the most popular websites offering LLC services at an affordable price. Their website is user-friendly, and every step is explained clearly, making the ordering process quick and easy. The starter package (valued at $39 for the first year and $119 after that) includes all of the essential products for LLC formation along with agent support, an operating agreement, and a risk-free assessment with one of their in-house certified public accountants (CPAs). Once you've selected your package, all you will need to do is provide some basic information about yourself and your business, and ZenBusiness will do the rest!

Use www.AutomatedRetirees.com/links/zen-business to get started!

TL;DR

Starting an Airbnb business is exciting and exhilarating! Like any business, you have to consider a lot of things to start off right. Most of the crucial decisions you have to make are based on:

How you plan on financing your Airbnb home

Your expected rental income once you have the property

Whether or not you will try to leverage debt

Once you have thought about those things, you need to check in with your local authorities and learn about any permits, licenses, and/or regulations you need to follow for short-term rentals. If your local laws are too strict, I'd suggest looking for another location offering more flexibility.

Oh, yeah, before I forget – you will also need to open a business. You can put it off, but if you want all the protections that come with an LLC, that LLC *must purchase* the property. So, you'll need to form it sometime before you sign any paperwork.

Whew! I'm glad we're done with selecting an area and finding a home. What a long chapter. Now, we get to the fun part: making money!

CHAPTER

Pictures & Listings & Reviews, Oh My!

———

"Make it simple. Make it memorable. Make it inviting to look at."

~ Leo Burnett

What You Can Expect in This Chapter:

- *Principles of design: creating the perfect atmosphere*

- *How to make your Airbnb guest-ready*

- *How to create a great listing*

- *How to increase your chances to get a 5-star review (and mitigate the 4-star-or-less reviews)*

Waiting With Bated Breath

I'll never forget the feeling of nervous excitement I had when I finally posted my Airbnb. I felt like I wanted to jump for joy and puke all at the same time. Thoughts raced through my mind, like, *What have I done?* And *Was this just an expensive mistake?* Or *At least we can use it for a vacation home!* Hey, not all investors are optimists!

But there I sat, in my Pinterest-worthy, newly furnished condo, contemplating my new hobby of looking at my phone every ten minutes to check for a booking. After half a day of nerves, I decided I needed a distraction. We flew to Florida from land-locked Austin, so we had to get some seafood!

My new hobby of checking my phone at 10-minute intervals continued, even after we sat down at the restaurant. But this time, something changed. *Ping!* The moment I had been visualizing for almost two months had finally happened. I got my first booking… and it was for three nights!

That was all it took to turn dinner into a celebration—and pull a 180 on the energy at the table.

Tips on Getting Your Airbnb Ready for the First Guest

If you've been following along, you now have a charming home in the perfect location. The next step is designing and furnishing it! When guests walk into your short-term rental, they need to feel like they are in a 5-star

92

retreat. You won't want your Airbnb to feel "lived-in"; you want it to feel like a chic hotel.

Contrary to popular belief, don't spend a fortune customizing your Airbnb. Design in the modern age isn't about gaudy gilded walls; it's about simplicity. And thank goodness – because simplicity is cheap.

If you're in desperate need of some inspiration, revisit your competition's listings. Airbnb makes it easy to see what your competition is doing. It doesn't matter if you don't have an eye for style; everyone knows good taste when they see it. If you like what you see, copy it! There's no shame in copying color schemes or furniture configurations.

Spying on the competition also gives you a baseline for what you need to do to make your short-term rental look up to snuff. If your space looks outdated – but so does everyone else's– then you can probably leave it as is. However, if you have a house built in the 90s and the area you're investing in has been gentrified… well, you might need to do a little upgrading.

The upgrades need not be expensive either. Something as simple as a paint job or swapping carpet for wood can make a dramatic difference in the place's overall aesthetics. And, *usually*, contractors can be paid with credit.

If you've never designed anything, you could try to bribe your friends into helping you. My dad was a godsend for my first Airbnb. He knew exactly what to do to make the space look amazing. If you don't have any friends who will help you, I have great news: my dad will!

I've included a list of all the things you should purchase for an Airbnb (everything from furniture to consumables) in *"Done for you: Furnish and Accessorize your Airbnb."* It not only includes what I use to furnish, accessorize and welcome my guests, it also includes links on where to buy them (and it's updated pretty regularly!)

Figuring out what you need to buy to decorate your Airbnb is just half the battle. You also need to figure out how to arrange it, so you give off the best vibes. Your maids will be responsible for this once they clean your Airbnb, but it's up to you to make sure you paint the walls and hang the pictures first.

Paint

Technically, you don't have to paint your walls if they are clean or have fresh paint already (unless you HATE the color!) Most hotels have white walls but make up for the blankness with colorful, abstract paintings. If you do paint your wall, make sure the rest of the room matches the color scheme. If it's a bedroom, the furniture and comforter have to match. The same goes for the living room and bathroom. In my opinion, white is just easier!

The downside to white is if the walls get smudged, you'll probably have to paint over it. It's very hard to clean white paint, especially if the paint is cheap.

Pictures

Paintings are a great addition to any room. I'm not talking about pictures of your family; I'm talking about the cheap paintings you can get from Amazon; they look stellar and can be pretty inexpensive. Hang prominent pictures on either side of your bed, above big pieces of furniture (like your couch). Accent your space with smaller pictures throughout.

Knickknacks

You don't need a lot of knickknacks throughout your rental. Your guests will rearrange and move them (for starters), putting more strain on your maid service because then they have to find them and reorganize them. For now – and especially if you don't have an eye for design – avoid knickknacks. *Hotels don't have them, so you don't need them either.*

TVs

Always buy smart TVs. Most guests have a Netflix or Hulu account they could use on their cell or tablet, but it's great if you provide a smart TV as part of your amenities. This gives your guests a great source of entertainment – and is almost expected nowadays.

TVs should always be hung on the wall. This makes it harder for guests to steal, and since Airbnb will not refund you for TVs, hanging them is the way to go. Thefts don't happen often, but let's try to avoid the remote possibility anyway.

Also, there's no need to buy the most expensive TVs or put them in *every* room. One large-screen TV in the living room should be just fine.

Bedrooms

Always center the bed on a non-windowed wall (typically, windows are on the wall to the right or left of the bed – not directly in front of it.) You will also need to buy two lamps and two end tables. Optionally, you could put another matching painting above your bed (if you don't have a headboard) or two medium-sized paintings above the end side tables.

Living room

Living rooms need a couch, two chairs, a coffee table, and a TV. Hang your TV on a wall without a window directly behind it - or on it. Your couch and chairs should form a square around the TV. The couch will face the TV, and the chairs will be up against the wall. Lay down a rug and put a coffee table on it (make sure the rug is not white because it will get stained!). You also want to make sure your coffee table is not made of glass because it's a pain to keep clean!

Optionally, you can place a tiny end table between the two chairs. If you do this, put a lamp on it.

If your couch is against a wall, hang a painting above it. Otherwise, you might not have space for any pictures – which is fine.

Kitchens

Everyone organizes their kitchen differently, but here are some helpful hints for your Airbnb. Have all of your kitchen items in a spot where your guests can see; knives on the counter, coffee machine near your source of coffee, pots and pans laid out neatly on a shelf, etc.

Coffee and tea (decaf, too), salt, pepper, and cooking spray are all things your guests expect when they stay at your Airbnb. These consumables are all laid out for you in the *Done For You Suite: Automated Consumables Shopping List.*

Dining room/Breakfast nook

Put the table in the center of the room with the chairs around it. Hang a painting on a wall, as long as the wall *doesn't* have a window. If all four walls don't have windows, then simply hang two on *opposing walls.*

Bathrooms

In your bathroom, have twice as many towels as you have guests (at full capacity). Remember: shampoo, body wash, and hand soap are all your responsibility, so don't skimp on those, either! Choose huge plastic bottles that squirt out body wash or shampoo; this – alone – will save you lots of money over time.

Picture day!

You bought your Airbnb, furnished it, and stocked it with consumables. There's just one more thing we need to do before we list: create our listing! That involves taking beautiful pictures and writing about all the reasons guests should book our property instead of someone else's.

1. Seriously, Clean and Detail Your STR With a Passion!

We've all visited a friend who has less-than-stellar standards for cleaning their house. Usually, the first thing you notice when you walk in is the smell… then the mess… then the dirt.

I've said it once (and yes, I'll say it again): Airbnb guests expect hotel quality. If they see a dirty tub or a stain on the counter, they *will* mention it. Usually, they'll do that in the reviews.

The same goes for photos. You might not realize it, but little details like dirt on the baseboards or a stain on the counter will be stand out - especially in pictures.

If cleaning is not your thing, hire a professional cleaning service for the initial, deep clean, and be sure to emphasize "hotel quality." Cleaning services that deal with Airbnbs regularly have a different standard than your everyday service, so it's even better if you hire them now. Heck, you might even get to meet the maids that clean your property regularly!

2. Remove All Personal Items

If your Airbnb home is also your vacation home, then you might leave personal items lying around. If those things live there full-time, pick them up and lock them in a safe hidden in your house.

Most Airbnb guests are honest people but as the Greeks say, *never tempt fate*! Besides, if you remove all your personal effects like pictures of your family, jewelry, cool custom surfboards, etc., your guests will feel more like they're at a hotel. That's what we want.

Here's a small list of things you should remember to remove:

- personal hygiene items
- clothing (or install locks on some closets and tell guests they are forbidden)
- technological devices like laptops, cameras, and phones
- jewelry
- personal documents
- family photos (replace them with cheap paintings from Amazon)

3. Add Your Own Special Touch

This topic is hotly debated in the short-term rental investor community.

What gifts, if any, do you leave for your guests?

Some people like to leave a bowl of fruit or a few wrapped chocolates. It's up to you and your profit margins.

For instance, if you want to budget $100 of fruit into your expendables budget and the numbers work out, then go right ahead!

Most Airbnbs have a few eggs, a small quart of milk, and an assortment of tea, coffee, (and decaf versions). If you know kids are coming, you can even stash some cereal in the pantry. If your guest is from out of town or another country, you could include some locally-made pastries or sweets.

Some new hosts immediately gravitate toward leaving alcohol out for their guests. I'd highly recommend against this, especially when you're taking listing photos. Not only is alcohol offensive to some people, but it's also a legal and liability issue. Plus, alcohol is an expensive gift, even if you just go for the $5 wine at Walgreens.

Overall, I'd recommend against it. Your guests won't expect it, so they won't be disappointed if it isn't there.

Taking Photos

You need not hire a professional photographer to take pictures for you. If you would like to hire someone to take stunning photos of your fully furnished property, it is usually somewhere between $100 and $200 to do the job. Just google "Interior Real Estate Photographer XXX city" and you'll find one quickly. They usually make sure the lighting is just right, pick out the best photos, and retouch them for maximum luxury.

I'd recommend you hire this job out. You only have to do it once, and it's well worth the time it saves you. You can expense it (think deductions at tax season) and can also use your 0% credit card to pay the photographer for the double whammy of points plus tax discount.

Before the photographer comes, make sure you...

- **Clean!** If you don't have the time to clean, hire a maid service to come in and do a thorough job. Pay attention to detail when you clean because any grease or stain can be easily seen in a picture. For example, clean your stovetops, deep-clean your carpets, and ensure there are no watermarks on surfaces because those show up – sometimes looking strange - on your pictures.

- **Take time to stage the room.** Beautiful staging can elevate the quality and appeal of a picture. If you need ideas on how to stage your room, then look at how other Airbnb investors in your area are staging theirs. Your photographer might help you, but that generally isn't in their job description.

- **Know what pictures you want.** When taking pictures for Airbnb, you want four for each bedroom (from each corner), one per bathroom, and two for every other room. You also want a nice photo of the front and back of the house – and the yard. Make sure the photographer knows this, so they add the photos you need for your packet.

f you'd rather not use a professional photographer, I have a few tips to help you take very professional-looking photos. The great news is that you can use any modern smartphone to take stunning pictures. Most newer phones even have necessary editing features within the camera or photos app. So, if you have a smartphone, put it to use by taking your own pictures! Do everything you would do *if a professional were coming* (clean, stage, and decide on which pictures you want) and consider the following tips.

How to Hold Your Phone

Hold your phone horizontally (landscape) and at hip level. Have your flash turned off (but all room lights turned on and all blinds or curtains open). Have the grid view and HDR turned on — this can be found in your settings. Last, tap on the screen before shooting so your photos are in focus!

Literally, Take 100 Pictures

As a novice photographer, you probably won't take a perfect picture every time. So, the more you take, the more likely you will find excellent ones! When you sit down to look at your photos later, you'll be able to tell which ones are great and which ones are just okay.

Editing Your Pictures

Selection

If you are like me and have trouble deciding, pick too many for your first round and whittle it down in subsequent rounds. Get some fresh eyes on the pictures. People might not know how to take great photos, but they'll know good ones when they see them!

Editing

You will most likely need to export your photos to some editing app – and many come standard with every computer. Find yours or go online and find a free one to get started. If you're absolutely terrible at this, you can go on www.Fiverr.com and pay someone to do it for you. It will probably cost you $1 per photo. Just search for "Real Estate Photo Editing."

To do this yourself, here are a few tips:

- Adjust the brightness, so your photos are bright. Make sure whatever your focus is on is the brightest. Don't go too far and make it look like it's a painting, but brighten that place up! One way you can do this is to turn up the blue saturation in your photos. There's something about seeing blue that makes humans feel light and fuzzy on the inside.

- Make sure the pictures are straight! Find something that was straight and straighten the photo based on that. It could be a tall lamp, a corner, or a door. Whatever it is, make your photo straight.

- Make sure nothing is glaring at you - no shiny bright spots.

- If your photos have points that are too bright, then adjust your highlight. You want a good balance between light and dark.

- Crop your photos to a 2:3 baseline - it's what Airbnb uses.

Once you have the photos you like ready to go, it's time to put them on your listing. Of course, you'll upload them a little later after you've created a great title and description. We'll go over this a little later when we talk about creating a listing. So, hang tight!

Writing a Stellar Listing

A Primer on Search Engine Optimization (SEO)

You've decorated, cleaned, taken pictures, and now you're ready for the customers to come rolling in. This next part is an important skill: the skill of search engine optimization. Since you're trying to make money with Airbnb, you are officially an *internet entrepreneur.* Congratulations! As an internet entrepreneur, you must learn how to do search engine optimization (SEO).

I know; it took me a second to wrap my head around it too. *Why should I care about SEO?*

SEO is the future for entrepreneurs. To sell anything online, you need to get good at SEO. It's right up there with learning how to advertise and write sales copy. I promise, once you learn a few key tips about SEO, you'll be able to sell anything online, not just Airbnbs.

What – Exactly – is Search Engine Optimization?

The internet runs on algorithms. These algorithms take the information you put in them and serve it up to other people they think may be interested in it. Companies like Amazon, eBay, Google, and Airbnb all use these algorithms! Their biggest concern is that they get the right ad in front of the right people. The better they get at that, the more money they make.

When you create an Airbnb listing, Airbnb tries to figure out who has the best chance of renting your STR. Airbnb is all about making money *for itself*. They don't care about you at all. So, the best thing you can do for your listing is . . . *make Airbnb money*. The only way you do that is by getting your STR rented as much as possible.

SEO is how you help Airbnb figure out who to serve your listing. You need to include specific words and phrases (known as *keywords*), so Airbnb has a good idea of who your property appeals to. The more people who choose to rent, the higher the occupancy rate. The higher your occupancy rate, the more money you make. The more money you make, the more money Airbnb makes because they take their cut out of your profits.

Who decides your occupancy rate? *The people renting your Airbnb*. I know that seems like a no-brainer, but it needs to be said. Some people see Airbnb as a money god, financially rewarding those with great listings. Airbnb has almost nothing to do with it! You are being rewarded by real-life people who decide to rent your STR.

People are looking through your pictures, description, and even your cancelation policy to determine if they want to stay with you. So, the better your sales copy, pictures, and amenities, the higher your occupancy rate.

In its simplest form, SEO is all about deciding which keywords are popular and writing a few paragraphs using those specific words.

Before we talk about what makes excellent keywords and super sales copy, let's talk about some basic things you can select from the platform to make your rental more tantalizing for your guests.

Writing and Optimizing Your Listing

Keywords

I love writing (can you tell?) So, naturally, I love writing sales copy for my Airbnbs. When I say sales copy, I mean the general listing. Most other Airbnb professionals will refer to the listing as the title and description, but to me, they're missing the whole point! This isn't just a title and description; this is your sales copy! It's how you will sell your Airbnb to your guest.

That's why I like to say *sales copy*; it gives the listing the gravity it deserves.

The more guesswork you can take out of your Airbnb business, the more profitable it will be. For instance, you absolutely cannot go with the flow to identify the target audience you hope to attract to your property. Why not? *When you try to appeal to everyone, you end up appealing to no one.*

Your home can't tick every box on every traveler's checklist. A businessman on a 2-night trip and a family on summer vacation expect two distinctly different experiences. The family might be looking for a little kitchen to cook dinner, a firepit to hang around, and a bunch of group activities in the city. A businessperson would prioritize a quiet place to work and delicious restaurants nearby that they could expense.

Your location will help narrow down your audience because it probably won't have all the attractions or amenities that every traveler is looking for. So, instead of being disappointed that not everybody will find your listing appealing, focus on the many people your listing appeals to – and fulfill their deepest travel desires!

Your Location

There are three major types of guests you could appeal to: families, bachelors, and businesspeople. Each of these customers will prioritize a different experience. Maybe they want to be close to an office? Perhaps your city has a cool zoo and some water parks. It's up to you to figure out what they will be attracted by in your city. Here are a few questions that will get you started:

- What kind of people live in your area? Is your area full of hipsters, corporate individuals, or families?

- What attractions are in your area or within close proximity? Is there an ocean, theme park, or huge conference venue nearby?

- What are the major festivals or conferences of your city?

- Will people visit in summer and winter?

- Where is your property located? Is it in a gated community? On a mountain? Downtown?

- Are there a lot of hotels in the area?

Three Major Guest Avatars

No, I'm not talking about the young guy with an arrow on his head or the blue aliens. An avatar is a representation of something. Here, it's a representation of our guest. I mentioned the three types of guests earlier, but I want to detail who they are here.

Family

If you've ever been on a family vacation before, then you'll have a good sense of what families like: good food at family-friendly restaurants, great sites like zoos, beaches, and theme parks (alternatively, campgrounds!) and – of course – some neat activities.

Adult

In my mind, "adult" represents an entire group. It might be a single guy who wants to tour the town, or it could be bachelor parties or huge groups of adult friends. Either way, these groups all want one thing: nightlife! They're coming to drink, make connections, and wake up after 2 pm.

Businesspeople

Businesspeople usually want to stay close to their office and expense all their food. They might have a drink or two, maybe they'll hit the bars, but generally, they need a quiet place to work.

<u>Your Property</u>

Once you have a good sense of your neighborhood, you can put together a plan for your property. However, your ideal guest will also need to be drawn in by your property. Below are a few questions you can ask yourself about your home to discover more about your typical visitor.

- What type of property are you offering?

- Is it a full house, condo, double bedroom, or couch?

- What amenities do you plan on offering your guests?

- Do you have a pool, covered parking, or free Wi-Fi?

- What makes your property different from the others on your street?

- Was your home built in modern times, does it have a lot of character, or is it spacious?

Now, let's build an example of a target audience analysis using these questions as guidelines and Anaheim, California, as our beach town destination.

1. Who lives in the area?

Families and blue-collar workers

2. What attractions are in the area or within close proximity?

Walt Disneyland, sports arena, conference center, the ocean.

3. Does the area have a broad or mass appeal?

This area has a broad appeal, with travelers visiting throughout the year.

4. Where is your property located?

About three blocks from the baseball stadium, less than 2 miles from Disneyland, and less than a mile from the conference center.

5. What amenities do you plan on offering your guests?

Free, uncapped Wi-Fi, barbecue grill, washing machine and dryer.

6. What makes your property different from the others on the street?

My property has more modern finishes, updated furniture, and more parking space.

<u>Searching for Keywords</u>

Now that you have a sense of who will stay at your Airbnb (or who you *wa*nt to stay at your Airbnb), you can collect some keywords! I like to use the tool https://smallseotools.com/keywords-suggestions-tool/. It's clunky but free. Most keyword tools cost between $100 and $300 per month, so remember that while you slog through it!

You need only to type in "Airbnb city/state/county." For instance, I would type in Airbnb Orlando Florida if I wanted to look at the keywords for Orlando, Florida.

This gives you a list of the top keywords for Airbnbs in that area. If any of them describe your listing, write them down! We're going to use them in our title and description.

Title

Unlike photos, I highly recommend you write your own title and description. I've spent a lot of money on Fiverr and Upwork, but I have yet to find someone who can write titles and descriptions as well as I can!

No one else will care about your business as much as you do – and great copywriters are expensive! Besides, most Airbnb hosts aren't getting their title right anyway. Heck, half of them are property managers who name the properties something convenient for THEM to remember, and the other half are people who haven't read my book—or any book for that matter. If I've convinced you to create your own title, then these tips will come in handy:

- **The first half of your title is the most crucial part.** People who view your title will probably whiz through it quickly to identify any keywords or striking information that makes exploring your listing worth it.

- **Take up all of Airbnbs characters.** You may want to write a short title, but a longer one will perform better due to search engine optimization. Writing a title is a careful balance between keywords and compelling copywriting. You need to appeal to both the Airbnb Algorithm and the potential guest. We'll go over a few examples later.

- **Use a symbol at the beginning.** Right now, people love little emojis when they're looking through titles. It's eye-catching and sets you apart from others.

- **List your top amenities in the title.** Does your property have amenities that you'd like to brag about? List these amenities (in an authentic *non-sales-pitch* kind of way).

- **DO NOT WRITE WORDS IN ALL CAPITAL LETTERS. NO ONE LIKES BEING YELLED AT.**

As I said, it's a careful balance between creating a title *stuffed with keywords* and one that appeals to potential guests. If your title is only one or the other, it won't work. We talked about finding keywords earlier. Let's say you know your keywords are "Private Room" "Near Campus" "6th Street". Those keywords appeal to the algorithm. But you can't just smash them all together; you need to shape them, so your title is pleasant to read. Imagine if you read a title that looked like this:

Private Room 6th Street Near Campus

It doesn't make very much sense at all! You'll have to dress it up so your guests have a clear idea of what you're selling.

🔥 Private Room Near 6th Street and Campus 🔥

This title comes off a lot better, giving potential guests a lot of information. They know they have a private room that will give them easy access to both 6th street and the campus. It's *definitely* better than what a lot of property managers call their properties.

Also, you don't have much space here; avoid too many adjectives and get straight to the point. It should go without saying, but don't lie about the type of property you're listing; it will cause a lot of bad reviews because your guests will be disappointed when they get there.

Description

The description is a lot like the title, just longer!

Descriptions should have pretty much every detail your guests want to know in straightforward language. Write this in a friendly, excited tone.

Avoid writing long essays saturated with adjectives and non-essential information. Have you heard of the SpongeBob effect? In short, nowadays, people are given everything so quickly that they don't have a very long attention span. You'll need to all but feed them the pertinent information as quickly as possible.

Let's talk about how you can do this in Airbnb and what information you need in different listing parts.

The "summary" is the part of the listing that appears right below the title – it's what the potential guest will read (if they read anything at all). This is your property's elevator pitch – make sure you have included bullet points about why your property should be booked! You can list features such as:

- The number of square feet in your property

- If there are captivating, private areas like fireplaces, pools, or decks

- Security features like garage parking for vehicles or a gated neighborhood

- Major landmarks and the time it takes to get to them (even better if they are within walkable distance)

- Always end with "Remarkably safe neighborhood!" because generally, all your guests prize their safety and security

When you get to "The Space" section, unleash your best-selling information. The point is to make the potential guest click on your listing and read more. Once they get to this section, they want more than just a summary; they want an in-depth explanation. When you get to "Guest Interaction," tell the guests how you will treat them. Are they going to check themselves in? Are you going to meet them at the door? Will you ever pop in? Look at other listings for more ideas.

Usually, only the most interested guests will look at the "Your Neighborhood" section because it's hidden under another layer of "click here for more information!" Don't overload your potential guests with a ton of things to do in your neighborhood; just add one or two bullet points for things they can do locally.

Once you reach the "Getting around" section, make sure to mention if your location is walkable or if they can use public transport. If neither of these is an option, let them know they'll need to use a rideshare service or rent a car.

IMPORTANT: You should not exaggerate about your property. Your description needs to be honest and have both the pros and cons of staying at your place. This is very important because you want your reviews to be as close to five stars as possible. You will not get five stars if you lie to your guests.

Photos

Now that you have fully-edited photos, you need to post them on Airbnb. Your main photo should set you apart from the others in your area – and you should have already determined that way back in chapter 3. Is it a bedroom? A picture of the nightlife? The front of the property? Decide which one sets you apart and put it first.

Once that's done, you must upload the rest of the photos. I recommend you put them in the order your guests would see them if they were touring your home. If they would start in a bedroom, put all four pictures from that one bedroom first. Then move to the hallway, bathroom, next bedroom, etc. End outside. Think of your Airbnb portfolio more like a virtual tour!

Captioning every photo helps the SEO and the guest! You'll want to write the caption in a way that the guest knows where they are in the home. Like "Master bedroom" or "Bedroom two." If all of your rooms look the same, this will help your guests determine where they are.

You also want to write your captions as if the guest is enjoying their time in your listing. For instance, you could say, "Imagine yourself lounging on the couch, IPA in hand, after a long day of touring the city!" It's a psychological trick that advertisers use – and you should, too. After all, you are advertising your investment; make sure each caption packs a punch because you only get about one sentence per photo.

110

Bnb Optimization Techniques
Get Rid of Maximum and Minimum Stay Requirements

Some guests like to plan their vacations around discounts, so they don't care so much about *when* they go; they just want a discount. Others have a set time that they'd like to stay in an area. Removing the max and min requirements for your listing will get your listing viewed by both of these guests!

There are a few reasons you might want to limit these.

Minimum Stay

Many hosts limit their minimum stay requirement to two days because it cuts down on locals who just want to use your STR as a party house. Parties are an enormous problem in Airbnbs right now. To that end, Airbnb has been known to de-list properties that have party complaints! There are other ways to avoid parties:

- Purchase a noise sensor. I've included this in my *Done for you: Furnish and Accessorize your Airbnb* list

- Tell locals "*No*" if they only want to stay for one or two nights

- Tell any guest that has a low-star or no-star rating "*No*"

An advantage to *not* having a minimum stay is that you open yourself up to more guests. Sometimes two guests will rent your STR a day or two apart; one may leave on a Friday, and the other will come on a Sunday. Without a stay-limit, you could rent your place to a guest on that Saturday in-between.

Maximum Stay

When you don't set a *maximum* stay requirement, you can attract medium-stay guests (guests who stay for more than one month but less than six months.) These are traveling businesspeople, traveling nurses, or anyone else who just needs a place to stay for a while. These guests are usually professionals, so they are a joy to handle, and they give you a month or two of 100% occupancy. That means less turnover!

The downside to longer stay times is squatters. Most states have a minimum required time in which a guest must stay to be considered a tenant. It's usually thirty days, but it can vary by state or country. If you have a guest who said they would stay for 30 days but doesn't leave when their time is up, you have to treat them like a tenant and evict them!

These long-stay visitors also have certain legal rights. For instance, you can't turn off the utilities to convince them to move – nor can you threaten them. You'll have to go through the entire eviction process. It's rare, but when it happens, it can turn into a nightmare.

Typically, you can avoid this by only allowing 4+ star guests in your home. You can ask them to sign a lease *in addition to* your Airbnb agreement (if they will legally become a tenant) just in case they surprise you and overstay their welcome.

If you don't want to deal with medium stay guests, you can set your max stay to just below the legal time limit for a tenant. Check your state's laws to learn about such time limits.

Increase the Booking Window on Your Listing

Some people only get a few weeks of vacation a year and need to plan it several months in advance. It makes sense to increase the booking window to attract these guests; six months is usually the sweet spot.

The only reason *not to do this* is if you temporarily converted your long-term rental to a short-term rental. If you're waiting on a long-term tenant, you probably want to stick to a 1-2 month booking window.

Add a Self-Check-In Option

Self-check-in is a must-have for the absentee Airbnb investor, allowing guests to come at their leisure and check themselves in. This automates the process for you and helps grow your business because you need not focus on day-to-day operations. Can you imagine having to check in five guests each day - manually? That sounds more like a full-time job than passive income!

Most Airbnb investors use a digital numbered door lock on their front door with a code that automatically generates for each guest. Some Airbnb investors use a lockbox system somewhere offsite. I'd recommend the former over the latter because guests find it easier. You'll just have to make sure your digital padlock is hooked into your Airbnb account so it can send your guests the combination before their check-in. https://www.remotelock.com/ is an excellent company with that type of lock. I highly recommend you check them out.

Some Tips for Better Communication

- Airbnb includes translation within the app, but it's always a plus if you already speak another language – especially if that language is common for tourists that like to visit your Airbnb. If you know how to speak another language, add this to your profile!

- Don't conceal any negatives about your property. It may seem like the wrong move to be upfront and talk about the flaws, but it's advantageous. Which is worse? Not booking a guest or having a guest give you a bad review because of an enormous inconvenience you forgot to share? Bad reviews are way worse!

- Send your guests a welcome message a few days before they arrive. I've included a basic welcome message package in my bonus package at the beginning of the book. Check it out if you want inspiration.

- Let the guests know that you are available for any questions they may have before they arrive. Most don't ask any; the ones that do will be infinitely grateful that you were responsive.

- Remember to send a check-out message a day or two after the guests leave. Mention that you will drop a great guest review; this encourages them to give you a positive rating as well.

More Tips to Attract Guests

- Accept pets! Yes, it is a personal choice, but hear me out. If your Airbnb has mostly hardwood floors, then pets are almost a no-brainer. Few Airbnbs allow pets because they worry that the pets will damage their property. This gives you an advantage because people with pets will flock to your Airbnb. Plus, you can charge a little extra. If the pets damage anything, just have your crew take a picture and send it to Airbnb for an insurance claim.

- Try and get Wishlist saves. It's a simple tip, but it's *gold*—people wish-listing your property signals to the algorithm that your property is worth renting. So, ask all your friends to Wishlist your property; it's free for them to do, and it might just push you to the top of the Airbnb rankings.

- Add more amenities to your Airbnb listing. If you are in a highly competitive market, then amenities could set you apart from other Airbnbs. At the very least, you want to make sure you have the *same* amenities that everyone else does. If you don't, it is a significant turn-off for most guests. That said, there is a point of diminishing returns. For instance, I would avoid pools or hot tubs if they aren't common in your area. Small additions like Netflix, Hulu, super-fast internet, etc., are more than appropriate. If you can, fire pits, outdoor movie screens, and massage chairs are also very popular additions that other Airbnbs might not have.

Don't decline or cancel bookings!

Airbnb will penalize you if you decline over three bookings for no reason. If a guest has horrible reviews, decline their stay (think of protecting your investment!) Also, if a guest breaks your rules, you can decline them without penalty.

How to Get Five-Star Reviews

Reviews are essential to both guests and hosts! For hosts, they seriously affect your ranking on the site. For guests, they impact their ability to instantly book an Airbnb.

Therefore, it's in both party's best interests to avoid bad reviews and collect as many good reviews as possible. Since this isn't a book about collecting good reviews as an Airbnb guest, I will just focus on hosting.

Review Box

Guests often use the review section in Airbnb to voice their concerns. That might be why a guest with a 4.9-star stay will take off an *entire star* for the tiniest problem. How do we fix this? We give our guests a place outside of Airbnb to voice their concerns.

This is simple. You have only to purchase a lockbox with a slit on the top or side and label it "Suggestions." Leave paper and pencils nearby so the guests can write their feedback about your place; this allows them to vent about those 1-star problems without taking off a star.

Excellent Customer Service

Airbnb investors aren't just in the real estate business; they're also in the hospitality business. In short: You're running a mini-hotel, and as you might guess, your guests expect a certain level of attention.

If the guest messages you during their stay with a query or concern, take them seriously. If you don't have an immediate answer, respond with "I see your text, and I am working on it now." Once you have had guests stay with you for a while, you'll have a list of questions and concerns they often ask. You can include them in your guidebook or have those answers saved in Airbnb's app... or both!

Strive to respond to the guest as soon as possible. Treat their problem as the most important thing in the world, no matter if it's something as innocuous as running out of firewood or as terrible as a leaky pipe. Let your guest know it's on the top of your mind and to-do list.

That doesn't mean you need to drop what you're doing and buy more firewood. It does mean you need to let your guest know that the problem will be resolved by xx time. *Of course, if it's something serious like a mini-flood, you probably want to take care of that immediately.*

Asking for a Review

You also want to make sure you send them a thank-you message after they leave; do it that night or the next day. Something like this works well:

> *Thank you for staying at my Airbnb! You were a great guest, and I hope you had a great time. Thanks for leaving the place in such great shape!*
>
> *Please don't forget to leave me a review. I'll be leaving a great review for you today!*
>
> *I hope you stay with me again the next time you visit.*
>
> *See you next time,*
>
> *Cat*

Make sure you *do* leave them a review! While they won't see yours until they leave their own, you must make good on your promise. If so, they're more likely to stay with you again – and might even tell their friends! That's called creating a following, baby!

You will also increase your guest's chances of having a great time with a stellar *message flow*. Your message flow should look something like this:

> **Immediately after booking:** *Booking confirmation.* Thank your guest for the booking, and provide the link to (and a pdf copy of) your guidebook.

Two days before check-in: *Check-in reminder*. Confirm their check-in time, state your check-in procedures, and remind them of your no-party policy. Make sure they affirm that they will not be throwing a party.

One day before check-in: *Welcome message*. Welcome them and make sure they're still coming. Send them anything they need to check in, including their code to the door. Reiterate parking instructions.

At the time of Check-in: *Check-in message*. Ask them if they had trouble checking in and if they need anything. Suggest somewhere nearby for dinner and let them know that they can ping you at any time.

The night before their departure: *Check-out procedures*. Send them your checkout procedure. Ask if there's anything they need.

Within two days of their departure: *Review Reminder*. We went over this above.

provide this template in my *Done For You: 5-Star Review Messaging Template*

Respond to All Reviews

Make sure you eventually respond to any reviews that guests gave you. If it was a four- or five-star review, highlight one or two things they said in our response and thank them. If it was a bad review, briefly address their concern and then state how it was resolved. Do not get defensive, but give guests perusing the review section a reason to trust you over your reviewer.

Creating a Guidebook

Most Airbnbs have a guidebook your guests can read to see all the information they need about the surrounding area. (I've created a sample guidebook for you in my *Done For You: Complete Guidebook Template*. Download it, so you have a template for your property. Everything you need to create one is included, so don't miss this!)

TL;DR

Posting your Airbnb is a feeling unlike any other! You're excited; you're nervous. You're ready to see if you've made a great decision (you have!) or a bad mistake. You realize that all the planning, strategizing, and crossing-of-fingers was worth it in the end.

At this point along the journey, your focus is on making sure your home is presented as the best version of itself. Suddenly, you are more aware of the competition and how they are operating their properties. Stalking your competition has a valuable purpose; it allows you to see areas where you can outdo them and offer an unmatched experience in your locale.

Part of creating this experience involves you preparing your property for guests and adding all the bells and whistles that will excite your expected visitors. It also means you now need to publicly share your listing online and optimize it to perform well on the Airbnb platform. You'll do that by employing SEO and amazing sales copy so your target audience both *sees* your listing and finds it irresistible.

We've covered the basics of Airbnb investing; now, let's get into some of the finishing touches to make your business shine!

Bonus: Final Touches

Confidence is a lot of this game or any game. If you don't think you can, you won't.

~Jerry West

What You Can Expect in This Chapter:

- *How to assess a guest*
- *A winning message flow that will prepare both you and your guests for your stay*
- *What makes for good house rules*
- *How to price your Airbnb for more bookings*

The Last Step

You've got your house, you've got your listing, and now, all you need is a little extra advice. I wanted to include a little bit more information in this short bonus chapter. There are a few things you don't think about when you decide to invest in Airbnbs. For instance, what makes a good house rule? What makes a good guest? How do I price my Airbnb? Then there's the coveted status of *superhost*.

I want to give you some passing advice on each thing before setting you loose to invest on your own!

Assessing a Guest

Reviews

When a guest wants to stay at your Airbnb, there are a few things you should consider. One of the major red flags is a review rating below 3-stars. I automatically pass on anyone who has that level of review. If they have a review rating between 3 and 4, I might read their profile to discover what happened to lower their rating.

Remember, people take off stars for small reasons sometimes. If a guest fell victim to a crabby host, I want to know about it!

120

References and a Complete Profile

If your guest has no reviews, then you must dig deeper. You will need to look at their profile and references to ensure they will treat your property respectfully.

A completed profile that has gone through the entire identify verification process is definitely a good sign. If they also have excellent references, I might be willing to take a chance on them.

Communicating Outside of Airbnb

All guest communications should be undertaken through Airbnb. No exceptions. It is a major red flag if your guests want to text, call your personal phone, or pay you using some other system. Airbnb has created an airtight system; everything you need to be a great Airbnb host is within its platform. If a guest wants to use some other system, tell them no.

You don't have to reject them if they wanted to use some outside system; after all, they might be new to Airbnb! But protect yourself at all times and follow Airbnb's policy of only using them to communicate.

Guests From the Same City

Guests from the same city as your Airbnb is a major red flag. Proceed with absolute caution because these guests probably want to use your property to host a party. We talked a little bit earlier about Airbnb de-listing properties if the neighbors complained about loud parties. This can – and does – happen. If you're desperate for guests to stay because you have no reviews, then you can book them. Just make sure you very clearly state that parties are not allowed.

House Rules

Creating great house rules is a necessary evil when investing in Airbnbs. It might feel kind of awkward writing your first *dos and don'ts* list for your prospective guests, but it's more than worth it. People would rather understand the rules than be surprised by a bad review later. And the more detailed you make your list, the better your guests will behave.

Here is the list of house rules I generally include in my packets:

1) No Parties!

2) Smoking areas (if you allow smoking)

3) Quiet Hours for the neighborhood.

4) The cleaning procedure the guests should follow before they leave (like putting their dirty dishes in the dishwasher or putting all towels in the washer.)

5) Absolutely no more guests than what they have included in the booking. If they have more guests than their booking states, you might not be covered under Airbnb's insurance.

6) Any off-limit areas in or around the home.

7) Any rules about the lights and heating. Should they turn the lights off before they leave each day? Do you have temperature controls?

8) Anything else that you can think of that would make life easier for your maids, guests, and neighbors.

Include these in your guidebook and laminate a copy, posting the laminate copy prominently – i.e., on the fridge or next to the TV. If you have Wi-Fi and your guests need a password, place the Wi-Fi password next to the rules (this increases the chance of your guests reading them!)

Pricing

When you start out, you want to have lower prices than everyone else in the area. No matter how well you wrote your title, how great your picture, or how amazing your description, guests will bypass properties with no reviews. Even one review is a significant improvement over none.

However, you can bribe them to take a chance on your listing if you have a lower price than anyone else in the area. It's human nature to look for a great deal, even if your guests are taking a chance.

This will lead to you breaking even or maybe losing a little money for the first month or two, but it's worth it! First, it will help Airbnb list your property at the top because more people are booking it. Second, after five reviews, you can raise your prices to about as much as everyone else.

Once you have those first five reviews, you can automate your pricing – and there are quite a few tools for this (Pricelabs, Wheelhouse, and Beyond Pricing). None are better than the others, so select the one you like the most. I use Pricelabs.co.

These tools aren't flawless (none are), so check to make sure they're changing your prices about once a week. This little change will significantly increase your bookings and thus your profits.

Your Base Price

You should have found this earlier when you were comping your property on Airdna.co or Mashvisor. Take 25% off the nightly rate until you have five reviews, then you can move it up to a higher price.

Listing Fee For Additional Guests

It's common practice for Airbnb investors to charge a little extra for more than two guests. It might seem rude to do, but it isn't! More guests in your Airbnb means more wear and tear. This takes a toll on your property eventually.

Charging for extra guests will also help keep your nightly rate low. You can charge a base rate of $60 per night and then upcharge $30 for each additional guest. It's standard practice; most guests expect this and are willing to pay it.

You can enforce this in mainly two ways. The first way is just to trust what your guest tells you. The second way is to install a doorbell camera and count the guests as they come in. I prefer the second way because it's a one-time purchase and helps you determine if the guests are paying fairly for the use of your property.

You can change this in Pricing, extra charges, and extra guest charges.

To deter more than two people staying in your Airbnb, you can make the charges for an extra guest something outrageous. *(I'm not sure why some hosts do that, but if you want to, for some reason, that's one deterrent.)*

To determine the charge per extra guest, just take your standard nightly rate and divide it by two. So, if you charge $60 for one night, then each extra guest is $30.

Remember, you can only have as many extra guests as your listing allows. To make your Airbnb amenable to many extra guests, place two beds in each bedroom and at least one bed in every other room. A sofa bed is an acceptable bed, as is a cot or fold-up stored in the closet.

If your guest count exceeds what your guest booked, file a booking charge with Airbnb immediately. This increases the chances of getting paid for those extra guests – and better than doing nothing at all. Please note: people just visiting for a few hours are not considered guests; staying overnight is the litmus test.

If your guest refuses to pay your extra booking charge, then you must file a resolution with Airbnb at www.airbnb.com/resultions. This is also where you can file a resolution for anything else – *including broken toilets.*

My Airbnb Is Not Booking

If you find that no one is booking your Airbnb, then you can do several things. My first recommendation is to lower your price by another $10. You never know, and $10 per night will make a huge difference to your potential guests. It might just be what you need to book it out!

Next, start looking more closely at your listing. Does it look nice? Is there some terrible typo discouraging potential guests? If so, fix it.

If you still aren't booking after that, it might be worth hiring a cohost or a property management company. But usually, the above two suggestions will help to book *any* Airbnb property.

How to Become a Superhost!

Superhosts get superpowers where SEO is concerned, as the algorithm will see you as a trustworthy host, sending your listing to the top of the heap! Guests also see you as trustworthy and might stay with you over someone else. This increases your occupancy AND the amount you can charge.

The good news is anyone can become a superhost, even if they have only one property. The bad news is that it does take some effort, and you can lose your status if you don't maintain these five points.

- Have at least ten bookings or three medium-term stays with a total of 100 nights booked in one year

- A 50% review rate - at least half of your guests left a review

- A 90% response rate - you respond to 90% of the prospective guest's questions within 24 hours

- Zero cancelations except in extenuating circumstances

- Have a 4.8-star rating

TL;DR

Once you make your first dollar from Airbnb, you'll be hooked! It takes long time to find, buy, and post an Airbnb, but in the end, it will all be worth t. At this point, you should know everything you need to know to become a uccessful host, whether it's selecting a great guest or pricing your property . . you can do it.

Definitely try to automate as many things as you can as an Airbnb host. One of those is the pricing! Automating your pricing strategy is the most critical thing you can do for your profits. Well, that and getting reviews! Almost everything else is just secondary.

Conclusion

———

A few weeks ago, my teenage brother, Brice, and I were taking a drive. He likes to talk with me about all kinds of subjects because - in case you haven't figured it out - I'm pretty fun to talk with! The subject at hand was *becoming rich*.

It disturbs me that most high schools don't talk to students about finances; it seems like our kids are growing up to be pawns in someone else's chess game; good little worker ants who save their money (or not) until they can retire at 70 (or not).

Brice and I discussed saving money; and how it *won't* make you rich. The discussion morphed into becoming wealthy. As described by the Maria Bonnano quote at the beginning of this book, true wealth involves freedom of time, not just a room full of gold. The only way you can do this is by creating value; you create value by investing wisely in either tangible assets or businesses.

This was a revelation to him, as it was to me almost five years earlier. It's a lot to chew on because it runs counterintuitive to what we are conventionally raised to believe. So, after a few moments of contemplative silence, he asked another question. *If it's that simple, why doesn't everyone do it?*

Arriving at this question is tricky. Most people just assume retiring early is impossible and don't even consider it. But when you ask why – and dig for the answer – you come to a startling conclusion.

People don't invest wisely because they're afraid.

They're afraid they'll make a poor investment choice – afraid they'll start a business that goes bankrupt. It might be fear of *failure* itself. After all, most people treat failure like some monster hiding just around the corner, ready to pounce and confirm your wildest suspicions: *you're a loser.*

If you're interested in the FIRE movement, then you must let go of your fear of failure. You need to realize that a poor investment will likely not be the end of the world, especially if it's in an LLC. Not to mention: everyone is new to *new stuff*.

Is investing in Airbnb scary? Yes. The first house you buy will have you skeptical in the least and shaking in your boots at the worst. You'll wonder why you chose to do this. You might even question your own sanity. Everyone does when they make a big decision. But you need to have the courage to go through with it.

Courage is not the absence of fear, but the triumph over it. The brave man is not he who does not feel afraid, but he who conquers that fear. - Nelson Mandela

Three million people are making money on Airbnb right now. If they can do it, why not you? How are you any different than them?

So, plant that tree. Take that leap. FIRE that job.

Be afraid, but buy that damn house anyway!

Trust yourself. It will all be worth it.

References

Abulatif, N. (2018, January 19). *Do You Need to Find a Real Estate Agent to Buy Investment Rental Properties? | Mashvisor*. Investment Property Tips | Mashvisor Real Estate Blog. https://www.mashvisor.com/blog/find-a-real-estate-agent-buy-investment-rental-properties/

Airbnb. (n.d.-a). *Are there any restrictions about what can be listed as a place to stay? - Airbnb Help Center*. Airbnb. Retrieved October 27, 2020, from https://www.airbnb.co.za/help/article/455/are-there-any-restrictions-about-what-can-be-listed-as-a-place-to-stay

All the Rooms. (n.d.). *The Best Apps For Airbnb & Vacation Rentals*. AllTheRooms Analytics. Retrieved October 30, 2020, from https://www.alltherooms.com/analytics/best-apps-for-vacation-rentals-airbnb/

Allen, J. (2020, May 13). *Rental Arbitrage: How to Make Money on Airbnb Without Owning Property*. Www.Biggerpockets.Com. https://www.biggerpockets.com/blog/airbnb-arbitrage

Berry, C. (2018, October 6). *New lending rule makes owning vacation property easier*. Mortgage Rates, Mortgage News and Strategy : The Mortgage Reports. https://themortgagereports.com/22394/new-lending-rule-for-second-home-vacation-property#:~:text=The%20rise%20of%20Airbnb%20and

BiggerPockets. (2019). How To Become A Millionaire Through Real Estate Investing (Newbies!) [YouTube Video]. In *YouTube*. https://www.youtube.com/watch?v=naZAknwNgkY

BiggerPockets. (2020). 8 Steps To Buying Your First Rental Property [YouTube Video]. In *YouTube*. https://www.youtube.com/watch?v=u83O2l1QEj4

Brumer, L. (2020, January 4). *The Pros and Cons of Being a Landlord*. Millionacres. https://www.fool.com/millionacres/real-estate-investing/rental-properties/pros-and-cons-being-landlord/

Bundrick, H. M. (2020, September 30). *Quicken Loans Mortgage Review 2020*. NerdWallet. https://www.nerdwallet.com/reviews/mortgages/quicken-loans-mortgage

Capital. (n.d.). *Low Risk Investment*. Capital.Com. Retrieved November 1, 2020, from https://capital.com/low-risk-investment-definition#:~:-text=An%20investment%20where%20there%20is

Christensen, K. (2020, June 24). *The Power of Leverage in Real Estate and How to Use It?* RealWealth. https://www.realwealthnetwork.com/learn/power-leverage-real-estate/

Clifford, R. (2017, January 12). *How to Automate Airbnb Messages*. Airbnb Smart. https://airbnbsmart.com/automate-airbnb-messages/

Clifford, R. (2020, March 21). *Airbnb Pricing Tools: Mega Breakdown [2020]*. Airbnb Smart. https://airbnbsmart.com/airbnb-automated-pricing-tools/

Danny. (n.d.-b). *Boost Your Airbnb Listing: Secrets From A Former Airbnb Employee • OptimizeMyBnb.com*. OptimizeMyBnb.Com. Retrieved October 29, 2020, from https://optimizemybnb.com/airbnb-listing/

Davis, G. B. (2018, May 9). *12 Secrets to Success for the New Airbnb Landlord*. SparkRental. https://sparkrental.com/12-secrets-to-success-new-airbnb-landlord/

Goodman, P. (2020, May 28). *The Pros and Cons of Being an Airbnb Host - ToughNickel - Money*. Toughnickel.Com. https://toughnickel.com/self-employment/The-Pros-and-Cons-of-Being-an-Airbnb-Host

GuestReady. (2018, April 11). *Why you should walk away from your Airbnb: The benefits of being a hands-off host*. Guest Ready. https://www.guestready.com/blog/hands-off-host/

iGMS. (2019, November 27). *Airbnb Rules: 6-Step Checklist to Stay Within the Law*. IGMS. https://www.igms.com/airbnb-rules/

Jasper. (2019a, August 8). *Airbnb Founder Story: From Selling Cereals To A $25B Company*. Get Paid For Your Pad. https://getpaidforyourpad.com/blog/the-airbnb-founder-story/#:~:text=It

Jasper. (2019, October 21). *63 Amazing Ideas to Make Your Home Airbnb Ready*. Get Paid For Your Pad. https://getpaidforyourpad.com/blog/make-airbnb-space-guest-ready/

Karani, A. (2019, March 31). *Buying Airbnb Property in 2019? Then You Need These 3 Tools | Mashvisor*. Investment Property Tips | Mashvisor Real Estate Blog. https://www.mashvisor.com/blog/buying-airbnb-property-2019-3-tools/

Karani, A. (2020, June 27). *A Guide to Financing Airbnb Properties | Mashvisor*. Investment Property Tips | Mashvisor Real Estate Blog. https://www.mashvisor.com/blog/financing-airbnb-properties/

Kline, K. (2019, August 27). *Why an Airbnb Listing Benefits Your Home or Vacation Rental Property*. Inc.Com. https://www.inc.com/kenny-kline/why-an-airbnb-listing-benefits-your-home-or-vacation-rental-property.html

Learnbnb. (2018, July 14). *How to Identify Your Target Airbnb Guest - PRO Tips*. LearnBNB.Com - Hosting Advice, Tips, & Resources. https://learnbnb.com/target-rental-audience-on-airbnb/

Lee-Joe, K. (2015, August 5). *How to prepare your home for Airbnb*. Domain. https://www.domain.com.au/living/how-to-prepare-your-home-for-airbnb-20150805-girulu/

Lily. (2017, October 27). *6 Biggest Reasons Why Airbnb Is So Popular | The*

Frugal Gene. The Frugal Gene. https://www.thefrugalgene.com/airbnb-popular/

LLC Formation Rocket. (2020, October 8). *3 Best Cheap and FREE LLC Services For Tight Budgets.* LLC Formation Rocket. https://llcformation-rocket.com/top-llc-services/#:~:text=For%20anyone%20looking%20for%20the

Maeva. (2019, August 29). *Airbnb Automation: Your Airbnb Business on Auto-Pilot.* Get Paid For Your Pad. https://getpaidforyourpad.com/blog/airbnb-automation-ultimate-guide/

Martinelli, K. (2017, February 23). *How to Pick a Location for a Vacation Rental Property | Futurestay.* Futurestay Blog. https://www.futurestay.com/read/holiday-rentals/management/location/

Norcom Mortgage. (n.d.). *Location, Location, Location: Why Location is so Important When Buying a Home. - Norcom Mortgage Blog.* Norcommortgage.Com. Retrieved October 28, 2020, from https://norcom-mortgage.com/blog/2015/01/20/location-location-location-why-location-is-so-important-when-buying-a-home/

Rented. (2016, November 4). *The Pros and Cons of Hiring a Vacation Property Management Company vs. Managing a Rental Yourself.* Rented. https://www.rented.com/2016/11/04/the-pros-and-cons-of-hiring-a-vacation-property-management-company-vs-managing-a-rental-yourself/

Rusteen, D. (2017, October 11). *How to Automate 80% of Your Airbnb Messages • OptimizeMyBnb.com.* OptimizeMyBnb.Com. https://optimize-mybnb.com/airbnb-automation/

Shalhout, S. (2018, March 4). *How to Find Low Risk Investments When Buying Rental Property.* Medium. https://medium.com/mashvisor/

how-to-find-low-risk-investments-when-buying-rental-property-e8b6c0362f65#:~:text=Look%20for%20a%20location%20with

Steven65. (2019b, January 10). *Why Location is important.* Community. Withairbnb.Com. https://community.withairbnb.com/t5/Hosting/Why-Location-is-important/td-p/909684

Stinson, B. (2018, March 22). *Airbnb Host Checklist for Room Designs.* Furnishr. https://furnishr.com/blog/airbnb-host-checklist/

Thrift, D. (2015, November 9). *018 Build Your Asset Column.* Real Estate Owned. http://www.drthrift.com/018/

Wang, K. (2016, January 10). *The Benefits of Being a Short-Term Rental Host.* Www.Igloohome.Co. https://www.igloohome.co/blog/rental-tips/benefits-of-airbnb-host

Weliver, D. (2020, October 16). *When Is It Better To Finance A Purchase Than Pay Cash?* Money Under 30. https://www.moneyunder30.com/finance-a-purchase-or-pay-cash

Yale, A. J. (2020, January 22). *Buying an Investment Property for Airbnb.* Millionacres. https://www.fool.com/millionacres/real-estate-investing/rental-properties/buying-property-airbnb/

Zaqout, K. (2017, November 30). *What's the Best Property Type for Short-Term Rentals? | Mashvisor.* Investment Property Tips | Mashvisor Real Estate Blog. https://www.mashvisor.com/blog/airbnb-apartment-vs-airbnb-house/

Made in the USA
Middletown, DE
31 August 2021

47330138R00077